The Disabilit
Carers Hand

The guide to your rights

Edited by Neil Bateman and Will Somerville

With chapters by

Neil Bateman
Chris Brace
Abena Dadze-Arthur
Kath Hoskisson
Mark Morrin
Donnia Reafat
Will Somerville

The Disability and Carers Handbook
The guide to your rights

Edited by Neil Bateman and Will Somerville

Published by the Centre for Economic & Social Inclusion
3rd floor, Camelford House
89 Albert Embankment
London SE1 7TP
Tel: 020 7582 7221
Fax: 020 7582 6391
Email: info@cesi.org.uk
Website: www.cesi.org.uk

Price: £14.95
ISBN: 1-870563-70-0

Disclaimer
Every effort has been taken to ensure the accuracy of the advice in this handbook. However, we cannot guarantee that the information contained is absolutely accurate. This is because guidance is constantly changing and as far as the authors are aware, all the chapters contain correct information at the time of writing.

Design: Stuart King & Linda Wilde, Landor Graphics, 020 8766 6539
Printing: Bath Press
Front cover: Peter Batt, Whizzywig, 020 8989 3341, www.whizzywig.co.uk

Contents

About this book

The Disability and Carers Handbook is a practical tool that details four distinct areas of welfare assistance that are available to disabled people and carers in an accessible format.

Part One deals with the financial support and benefits available, explains what the eligibility criteria are, the routes and administrative processes in play when accessing them, and the different choices the individual has in deciding how to receive them.

Part Two sets out the employment and training programmes that are designed specifically for disabled people as well as other relevant provision, including current pilots and the recently introduced Work Focused Interviews process. This part also covers financial support available to help you through any transitional periods when moving from receipt of welfare assistance into paid employment.

Part Three details the Disability Discrimination Act (DDA), and how this operates, including the latest developments regarding access to services and what employers must offer disabled people in the workplace. Examples are given of the types of practical measures that can be introduced in the workplace and how the 'Access to Work Scheme' can help you and your employer with financial support.

Part Four looks at some common issues and concerns. This part includes how best to negotiate access and find out about rights to community care services, maintaining benefits access when going into hospital and how to receive help with residential care.

The Handbook includes a CD Rom, containing a database of useful organisations and contacts.

Our Further Information section will also help you identify contacts and reference sources for further reading.

The index at the back of this book gives page references and allows you to search by specific topics and key words, including all relevant benefits, programmes and organisations.

Introduction

It has been estimated that in Britain there are 9.8 million people with a disability and 5.7 million people who spend at least some time being a carer.

If you have a disability or a long-term health problem, or you are a carer, negotiating a way through the benefits system and maximising income is a vital part of addressing poverty and social exclusion. The Benefits system also offers an essential gateway to enter or access various government programmes to help people with a disability into work or training.

This Handbook is the latest in a series published by *Inclusion,* designed to be introductory level guides to benefits and training rights for key groups of people who experience poverty and social exclusion. Practically, it is aimed at advisers and practitioners.

The key benefits for people with a disability are outlined in sufficient detail to enable the reader to identify most underclaimed benefits and to tackle many common benefit problems. Readers are also be guided through the maze of projects and schemes to help people with a disability or long-term health problem get a foothold in the labour market and possibly enter part or full-time employment.

While we have taken every effort to ensure that the contents of this book are accurate, there are often exceptions and other situations where the advice in this book will not apply. This is not a comprehensive guide to welfare rights and inevitably there are gaps in what is covered and many areas have been simplified in order to make the subject accessible to a wide readership. Readers should seek advice themselves to supplement the general guidance contained in this book.

Part One: Financial support and benefits
Neil Bateman

Chapter One: Approaches to welfare rights work

There are a number of effective approaches to welfare rights work. These approaches can reduce the frustration of dealing with often remote bureaucracies.

First, some ethical principles for effective advocacy:

- act in the service user's best interests
- act in accordance with the user's wishes and instructions, if they have capacity
- keep the user properly informed
- carry out instructions with diligence and competence (recognising your own limitations)
- act impartially and offer frank, independent advice
- maintain confidentiality.

Things to remember

- always personally check the correct rules and interpretation
- use this book to identify benefit entitlement and then refer to the more specialist books mentioned in the text, keep up to date by reading, having up to date reference books, and attending training

- build up a network of experts whom you can call on for help and support. Don't be embarrassed to call on them for advice – none of us knows it all

- view welfare rights problems as inter-related and avoid tackling issues in isolation from one another

- try to carry out a check of all benefit entitlement as a routine part of any assessment or when any financial issue is presented. This is a good way to spot if someone is, for example, underclaiming for a benefit

- avoid negotiating by phone and it is best to confirm things in writing

- don't get overwhelmed by what seem to be impossible problems - all problems have some kind of solution and you may need just a small amount of help to find it

- the social security system uses National Insurance (NI) numbers to identify benefit claimants. People without an NI number can be helped to apply for them and should receive a payment on account of their benefit while they wait for an NI number. Keep a record of NI numbers and include them in communications with the Department for Work and Pensions

- gather supporting evidence for any argument from a variety of sources and present it in a way which supports the best rights interpretation

- it is often well worth the time to fill in claim forms – particularly for Disability Living Allowance and Attendance Allowance. Even the best of us can find forms daunting to fill in unaided, let alone if you're experiencing poor self-esteem, turmoil, stress, or if English is not your first language

- keep your interviewing skills sharpened and record important and useful facts that might have a bearing on benefit entitlement
- build up your assertiveness skills
- develop skills in researching a case and finding the most favourable argument
- remember the power of rights which are enforceable by appeals and don't shy away from using these
- never fib in order to try to get round benefit rules, but honestly present the facts in the best light. Never help people with completing a form, letter or phone call which includes facts that you know are untrue. If in any doubt, seek independent advice
- seek specialist help in any fraud cases or if you suspect a service user is participating in fraudulent activity. With the latter, advise them of their duty to report relevant information to the benefit authorities and record that you have given this advice, even if they choose not to take it – in which case you have the option not to assist them.

Where to get help

There are several ways you can get help with welfare rights problems. First ensure that you have copies of this book. Also ensure that you have access to an up to date edition of the Child Poverty Action Group's Welfare Benefits and Tax Credits Handbook and the Disability Alliance's Disability Rights Handbook. *Inclusion's* other guides – The Young Person's Handbook Second Edition, Welfare to Work Handbook Second Edition and The Newcomer's Handbook, complement this book.

In many areas there are welfare rights services which can provide help and advice, however, the distribution and location of these services varies and some concentrate on casework, others on training.

There are an increasing number of useful websites, including government ones where you can download claim forms for most benefits and tax credits

A long list of useful websites is available on the CD Rom and the further information section at the back of this book.

Chapter Two: An outline of the benefits system

The United Kingdom's benefits system is based on a combination of contributory benefits with entitlement based on National Insurance records, non-contributory benefits with entitlement based on meeting the eligibility criteria (neither income, capital nor the National Insurance record is usually significant) and also on means-tested benefits with entitlement based on detailed eligibility criteria and rules about income and capital. Some benefits are also now paid via the employer (i.e. Statutory Sick Pay and Statutory Maternity, Paternity and Adoption Pay).

In recent years we have had the development of Tax Credits which are a form of income maintenance based on social security principles but paid by the Inland Revenue.

Finally, there is a range of education and health benefits that are administered by local authorities and the National Health Service (Education and Library Boards and the Health Service in Northern Ireland).

There are strong relationships between one benefit and another and so it is best to view the social security system as a jigsaw with pieces which fit with others because entitlement to one benefit can sometimes be based on entitlement to another benefit. This is so that particular groups can receive additional help – for example, people with children or people with a disability, and is commonly referred to as 'passporting'.

Benefits at a glance

Contributory benefits	Non-contributory benefits	Means tested benefits and tax credits	Employee benefits
Retirement Pension ❤◆▲	Disability Living Allowance	Income Support	Statutory Sick Pay ▲
Incapacity Benefit ❤◆▲	Attendance Allowance	Jobseeker's Allowance ❤	Statutory Maternity Pay ▲
Jobseeker's Allowance ❤▲	Child Benefit	Pension Credit	Statutory Paternity Pay ▲
Maternity Allowance ▲	Industrial benefits	Child Tax Credit	Statutory Adoption Pay ▲
Bereavement Allowance ▲	War pensions	Working Tax Credit	
Widowed Parent's Allowance ▲◆	Carer's Allowance ▲◆	Housing Benefit	
	Incapacity Benefit (non contributory)/ Severe Disablement Allowance ◆❤▲	Council Tax Benefit	
		Health benefits	
		Social Fund	
		Education benefits	

❤ - There are both contributory and non-contributory versions.

◆ - There are Child Dependency Additions to these benefits, but only for people receiving them before 7th April 2003. Claims made after this date will be treated as a claim for Child Tax Credit.

▲ - These benefits are covered by the overlapping benefits rules. These mean that you can only receive the highest of whichever one they qualify for.

Who may receive what

The following list gives some broad indications of the various benefits for different groups of people. People often receive a combination of benefits and may be unclear about which benefits they receive. People must meet the conditions of entitlement for each benefit/tax credit.

Older people (aged 60+)	Sickness or disability	Carers
Retirement Pension	Statutory Sick Pay or Incapacity Benefit	Carer's Allowance
Attendance Allowance and/or Disability Living Allowance	Severe Disablement Allowance	Income Support
State Pension Credit	Disability Living Allowance	Child Tax Credit
Housing Benefit	Income Support	Housing Benefit
Council Tax Benefit	Housing Benefit	Council Tax Benefit
Carer's Allowance	Council Tax Benefit	Health benefits
Bereavement Allowance	Industrial injury benefits	Education benefits
Health benefits	War Pension	
Education benefits	Child Tax Credit	
Winter Fuel Payments	Working Tax Credit	
	Health benefits	

Unemployed or part time work (less than 16 hrs per week)	Full time work (more than 16 hrs per week)	People with children	Bereavement
Jobseeker's Allowance Income Support (if not required to be available for work and to sign on, for example, lone parents) Child Tax Credit Housing Benefit Council Tax Benefit Health benefits Education benefits	Working Tax Credit Child Tax Credit Housing Benefit Council Tax Benefit Health benefits Education benefits	Child Benefit Child Tax Credit Working Tax Credit Education benefits Health benefits All other benefits	Bereavement Allowance/ Widow's Pension Widowed Parent's Allowance/ Widowed Mother's Allowance Bereavement Payment Income Support Housing Benefit Council Tax Benefit Child Tax Credit Working Tax Credit

Who administers what?

Welfare benefits in the UK are administered by various central and local government departments. There are a few minor differences in Wales, Scotland and Northern Ireland. However, the same social security rules apply throughout the UK and the only differences arise with non-social security benefits (e.g. NHS benefits and home insulation grants). In Northern Ireland there is no Council Tax and the rate rebates system still operates.

In Great Britain, the Department for Work and Pensions administers benefits through the Pension Service, Jobcentre Plus and the Disability and Carer's Service. Jobcentre Plus is being rolled out across the country so that by 2006 all areas will have Jobcentre Plus services which will integrate jobseeking and benefits administration services. For simplicity 'Jobcentre Plus' is referred to, this reference also includes services provided by old style Jobcentres and Social Security offices.

In Northern Ireland, benefits are administered by the Department of Social Development's Social Security Agency with Housing Benefit administered by the Northern Ireland Housing Executive.

Some benefits are administered in large national or regional units and some of the latter may be a considerable distance from the actual locality they serve.

The following shows where the main different benefits are administered in Great Britain.

Benefit	Where administered
Attendance Allowance	DWP Disability and Carer's Service, regional offices (new claims) Existing claims: Disability Benefit Unit Government Buildings, Warbreck House, Warbreck Hill, Blackpool, Lancashire FY2 Tel: 0845 712 3456 Fax: 01253 331 266 Textphone: 0845 722 4433 To obtain a claim pack: 0800 882200
Bereavement Benefits	DWP Jobcentre Plus local office
Carer's Allowance	DWP Disability and Carer's Service, Palatine House, Lancaster Road, Preston, Lancashire PR1 1HB Tel: 0177 289 9655 Fax: 01772 899 354 Email: ICA-Customer-Services @dwp.gsi.gov.uk
Child Benefit	Inland Revenue, Child Benefit Centre, (Washington), PO Box 1, Newcastle-upon-Tyne NE88 1AA Tel: 0845 302 1444 Textphone: 0845 302 1471
Council Tax Benefit	Local authority responsible for housing services usually located in the council's finance service)
Disability Living Allowance	DWP Disability & Carer's Service, regional office (new claims). Existing claims: Disability Benefits Unit, Government Buildings, Warbreck House, Warbreck Hill, Blackpool, Lancashire FY2 0YJ Tel: 0845 712 3456 Fax: 01253 331 266
Education Maintenance Allowance and Welsh Assembly Learning Grant, free school meals and school clothing grants	Local authority responsible for education services. EMAs after September 2004: 0845 60 222 60
Housing Benefit	Local authority responsible for housing services (usually located in the council's finance service)
Incapacity Benefit	DWP Jobcentre Plus local office

Benefit	Where administered
Income Support for people under 60	Department for Work and Pensions (DWP); Jobcentre Plus local office www.jobcentreplus.gov.ukDWP Jobcentre
Industrial benefits	Jobcentre Plus local office
Jobseeker's Allowance	DWP Jobcentre Plus local office
Maternity Allowance	DWP Jobcentre Plus local office
NHS benefits	Agency Benefits Unit. Contact: DWP Jobcentre Plus local office
Pension Credit	DWP regional Pension Centre www.thepensionservice.gov.uk Application line 0800 99 1234
Retirement Pension	DWP regional Pension Centre New State Pension claims 0845 300 1084 Textphone 0845 300 2086 (8am-8pm, Monday-Friday) www.thepensionservice.gov.uk
Social Fund payments and Sure Start Maternity Grants	DWP Jobcentre Plus local office
Statutory Sick Pay, Maternity, Paternity or Adoption Pay	Employer, but disputes dealt with by local Inland Revenue office
Statutory Sick Pay	Employer, but disputes dealt with by local Inland Revenue office
Tax Credits	Inland Revenue, New claims: 0845 300 3900 Textphone: 0845 300 3909 www.taxcredits.inlandrevenue.gov.uk
War Pensions	Veterans Agency (Ministry of Defence) Norcross, Blackpool FY5 3WP 0800 169 22 77 Textphone 0800 169 34 58 help@veteransagency.mod.uk or via local War Pensioner's Welfare Service www.veteransagency.mod.uk

Getting paid

The government's preferred method for paying all benefits and Tax Credits is direct into a bank account (known as 'Direct Payment'). All banks and most building societies now have basic accounts which are specially designed for people on very low incomes. The Post Office also offers a card account specially designed to only receive benefit payments. It is possible to withdraw payments from these accounts and from some current accounts over the counter at Post Offices, but the requirement to use an electronic keypad and a PIN is difficult for some people. The compulsory use of direct payments is being phased in and there is concern that some people will have difficulty in opening or operating basic accounts – for example, those who are bankrupt, vulnerable young people, people without an address and people with chaotic lifestyles. The DWP can arrange payment by cheque in such cases.

If you need someone to collect your money for you, this can be arranged with the bank, building society or Post Office, but if the person collecting changes (for example, there are several home-carers), the process is difficult to operate and requires safeguards against third party misuse.

At the time of writing, Housing and Council Tax Benefits can't be paid into a Post Office Card Account because of technical and contractual difficulties.

Tax Credits can only be paid into an account but it is possible for them to be paid by cheque in exceptional circumstances. Use the exceptional circumstances argument if you find difficulty with managing accounts and seek independent advice if refused.

Most benefits are paid weekly but Jobseeker's Allowance and Incapacity Benefit and some payments of Income Support are paid in arrears (the first two being paid fortnightly in arrears). It is possible to have weekly payments if fortnightly payments causes particular difficulty but Jobcentre Plus may resist this – seek independent advice.

Sometimes payments are lost or paid into the wrong account before they reach the right person. It is possible to take legal action to enforce payment in such cases as the DWP are usually very slow to replace lost payments or may even refuse to. If people lose money after cashing a cheque or after withdrawing from their account, the DWP are under no obligation to make up the shortfall but a Social Fund crisis loan may be payable.

If you are unable to manage your benefit, it is possible for someone to apply to be an appointee who then legally takes on all your benefit responsibilities – making claims, reporting changes of circumstances, repaying overpayments and collecting payment to be spent on behalf of the person on benefit. The DWP have been known to insist that someone has an appointee but no one can be forced to have one (for example, if there is no one suitable to become an appointee) and they should regularly review whether or not someone still needs an appointee – this is a particular issue for adults with a learning disability who could achieve financial independence. You can make representations about appointeeships and they should be terminated by the DWP if the appointee is misspending money. An appointee can also resign if they want to. A claim for a benefit should not be refused nor held in abeyance if someone is not willing and able to take on the role of appointee.

A corporate body can be an appointee (for example a local authority, housing association or an NHS Trust). This protects individual staff who may otherwise be personally liable to repay overpayments if they become an appointee.

A separate appointeeship must be made for Housing and Council Tax Benefits. Seek advice if someone has a power of attorney or is a receiver for the Court of Protection or acts under similar powers in Scotland.

Claims and appeals
(different rules apply to War Pensions)

All benefit claims should be made on the correct application form. However, if a claim has been made in another format, (for example, a letter or an incomplete claim form), you have one month to complete the form and the claim dated from then (longer if you have a good reason for a delay). This also applies where supporting evidence or information is required. The one month period can be extended if 'it is reasonable' to do so but does not apply to Pension Credit.

The following can be claimed on-line: Child Benefit, Carer's Allowance and both tax credits.

For Housing and Council Tax Benefits, the date of claim is the date when a completed claim form is returned to the local authority. However, if a letter or phone call is made to request a claim form, you can ask for a claim to be backdated to the date of first contact.

For Jobseeker's Allowance claims from couples without children, if at least one of the couple was born after 28 October 1957, both members of the couple must normally make a joint claim unless one is working more than 16 hours a week.

The law also requires that once a benefit claim has been submitted in the correct format, a decision must be made on it by a Decision Maker within 14 days unless it is not reasonably practicable to do so. Powers exist for interim payments of benefit to be made. For private tenants who have made a claim for Housing Benefit, it is a legal requirement that an interim payment must be made if your claim can't be processed within 14 days and you have not caused the delay.

If there is a delay in making a decision, it may be possible to take legal action to have a decision made and if a DWP benefit payment is delayed for more than three months, it may be possible to obtain compensation – seek advice. Housing Benefit delays may also be reported to the Local Government Ombudsman and legal action may be possible if you have suffered harm or loss because of delay. However, these rules do not apply to tax credits and the Inland Revenue operates a system of emergency payments when there are delays.

Backdating benefit claims

Benefit claims can be backdated in certain circumstances. It is important not only to make sure that claims are made but also to ask for backdating if entitlement has existed for some time. Benefit claims will not be backdated unless requested.

There are different rules about backdating different benefits. Claims for some benefits may be treated as claims for others (known as a 'claim in the alternative'). For example, a claim for Maternity Allowance can be treated as claim for Incapacity Benefit and vice versa and a claim for Disability Living Allowance treated as a claim for Attendance Allowance and vice versa. A claim for Income Support can be treated as a claim for Carer's Allowance and claims for Income Support and Pension Credit can be treated as claims for each other. This means that a claim for a benefit may be backdated to the date of an earlier claim for another benefit.

Some benefits can be backdated without having to show any special reasons, just previous entitlement, for up to three months. These are: Incapacity Benefit, industrial injuries benefits, Child Benefit, Guardian's Allowance, Pension Credit (which can be automatically back dated to 6 October 2003 if claimed before 6 October 2004. After this it can be backdated 12 months), Retirement Pension, bereavement benefits (the Bereavement Payment can be backdated 12 months), Maternity Allowance, Carer's Allowance and Tax Credits.

Income Support and Income-Based Jobseeker's Allowance can be backdated up to one month in specific circumstances (for example, a close relative died, transport difficulties to the DWP office, or separating from a partner). These benefits can also be backdated for up to three months where there are 'special reasons'.

If your benefit depends on (or a higher rate depends on) an award of another qualifying benefit, then most benefits can be backdated to the date that the qualifying benefit was awarded, provided that the benefit was claimed before the result of the claim of a qualifying benefit is known and then a further claim is made within three months of being awarded the qualifying benefit. Seek advice in such cases, as this is a very brief summary. It will mostly apply to means tested benefits.

Housing Benefit can be backdated for up to 52 weeks if the person can show that they have continuous good cause for claiming late. This is very broad and a wide range of circumstances can qualify.

Changes and challenges to benefit decisions

It is possible to challenge a benefit decision in a number of ways:

- by an appeal
- by a revision and/or
- by a supersession.

Appeals

An appeal must be submitted in writing (on DWP form GL21, Inland Revenue form WTC/AP for Tax Credits or by letter in a similar format), within one month of the decision that is being appealed against being posted to the claimant. This period can be extended by 14 days if the claimant asks for a statement of reasons about the decision they wish to challenge. If the DWP or local authority revise the decision after an appeal has been submitted, the appeal will lapse. Note that a further appeal may be necessary if the new decision is only partly favourable.

Appeals are heard before a social security Tribunal which normally consists of one member, the Chairman, who is a lawyer or barrister. Appeals about Attendance Allowance and Disability Living Allowance are heard by a Chairman, carer member and doctor. Incapacity Benefit and industrial injuries Benefits appeals are heard by a medically qualified Tribunal member and a Chairman. There are no costs for appealing to a Tribunal and proceedings are fairly informal.

It is essential to obtain specialist help and representation if at all possible. If unsuccessful, a case heard by a Tribunal can be appealed to the Social Security and Child Support Commissioners and thence to the Court of Appeal and House of Lords. Decisions of the Commissioners and Courts set binding precedents on Tribunal and benefit decision makers.

The Government plans to eventually transfer all appeals about Tax Credits to the Tax Commissioners. As well as appealing to a Tribunal, Tax Credit decisions can also be challenged by making a complaint to the Inland Revenue Adjudicator.

It is possible to appeal more than one month after a decision has been sent out but only in limited circumstances and then only with the permission of a Tribunal Chairman. The grounds for late appeal are:

- the appeal has been made less than 13 months after the original decision was made
- there is a reasonable prospect of it succeeding
- and either it is in the interests of justice to grant your request or there are special circumstances why you haven't appealed within the time limit.

It is therefore important to submit all appeals within one month as far as possible because many late appeals will not be allowed to be heard, whatever the strengths of the case.

Sometime after an appeal has been submitted, the person who has appealed will be sent a form (TAS 1) to complete and return within 14 days. If they don't do this, their appeal can be struck out (though it can also be reinstated). It is not unknown for representatives to not be sent this form.

Revisions

You can ask for a benefit decision to be revised within one month of the decision being posted. It is also possible for the benefit decision maker to revise his or her own decision at anytime. If you do not ask for a revision within one month, you can ask for a late revision.

If a decision is not revised favourably then it can be appealed, provided this is done within another month. Revisions are particularly useful in Disability Living Allowance and Attendance Allowance cases as you can ask for the rate being paid to be varied if it is felt to have been incorrect or too low. However, if you seek a revision of these benefits, the whole claim is examined and in borderline cases, it may result in someone's benefit being reduced.

Supersessions

A decision can be superseded at any time by a Decision Maker if there has been, or there is likely to be, a relevant change of circumstances since the decision.

Decisions can also be reviewed when the original decision was made in ignorance of a material fact, was based upon a mistake or was based on an error in law. Such a supersession can happen after a revised decision or if a decision has been appealed.

If a benefit decision is superseded, any change in payment only takes effect from the date of the supersession (not the original claim date). But if you notify the DWP within a month about a change of circumstances, then it can be paid from the date of the change of circumstances.

Housing Benefit

A parallel system of revision, supersession and appeal exists for Housing Benefit with appeals also being heard by a social security Tribunal. A Housing Benefit appeal needs to be made in writing but not on a special form. There have been serious delays in local authorities passing on appeal papers to the Tribunal Service and it may be possible to take legal action or to complain to the Local Government Ombudsman about this.

It is possible to both appeal and also apply for a revision. In addition, in cases of poor administration, particularly when inconvenience, hardship or loss has occurred, one option is to contact the Local Government Ombudsman within a year of the issue arising. The Ombudsman has powers to call for documentation which would not otherwise be available to the complainant, and so this system is best where a critical scrutiny or investigation is required. Investigations take about a year to conclude. The Ombudsman can recommend compensation, but the authority does not have to accept the recommendation (it is unusual if they don't).

Another option in a serious situation where the bureaucracy seems impenetrable is to write to the Monitoring Officer (MO), (all authorities must have one), with an account of why the situation is believed to be a breach of the law. The MO is obliged, under the Local Government and Housing Act 1989 to give personal consideration to the situation, and if s/he agrees that a breach of the law has been identified, a report must be prepared and circulated to all Members. This is therefore a quick, free and direct way of getting the urgent attention of elected councillors and senior management when a problem seems to be insoluble.

People coming from abroad

This book assumes that you will not have difficulty receiving benefit because of your immigration, nationality or residence status. Many people coming from abroad face restrictions on receiving benefit, either permanently or for a limited period. The Habitual Residence Test in particular can cause difficulties for people not long in the UK who claim means tested benefits.

This is a complex area and is covered in *Inclusion's* Newcomer's Handbook and the CPAG Migration and Social Security Handbook. It is important to have these books if you are caught by such rules and to also obtain specialist independent advice.

Chapter Three: Benefits for disability and ill health

Disability Living Allowance and Attendance Allowance

What are they?

Disability Living Allowance (DLA) is a benefit for people under 65 who have a physical or mental disability (including mental illness, learning disability and behavioural problems). It can be awarded to children or adults. It is not means-tested, is tax-free and is paid on top of other social security benefits. It has two components, one for care and the other for mobility and there are three care component rates and two mobility component rates. It is paid to people who need help looking after themselves or who need someone on hand in case of danger and/or who find it difficult to walk or get around.

Attendance Allowance (AA) is the equivalent of the DLA middle or higher rate care component for people who claim after age 65 but it is paid at two rates instead of three (there being no equivalent to the lower care component rate of DLA) and there is no mobility component.

Disability Living Allowance (DLA)

Who is entitled?

You must be aged:

- 0 - 65 years for the care component

- 3 - 65 years for the mobility component (5 years or over for the lower mobility component rate). If it is awarded, it can continue to be paid after the age of 65, provided that the person still meets the rules for getting it.

You must also have needed help or had mobility problems for at least three months and the condition must also be likely to last for at least six months, unless you qualify under the special rules for people with a life limiting illness.

Care component (three rates):

Higher rate (day and night attention or supervision)

You must need 'frequent attention throughout the day with your bodily functions', or 'continual supervision to avoid substantial danger to yourself or others'.

and

At night you need 'frequent or prolonged attention with your bodily functions', or 'someone to be awake for a prolonged period or at frequent intervals for the purpose of watching over'.

Middle rate (day or night attention or supervision)

You must satisfy at least one of the above conditions for attention or supervision during the day or the night.

Lower rate

You need attention with bodily functions for a significant portion of the day, or (if 16 or over), must be unable to prepare a cooked meal if you have the ingredients.

Mobility component (two rates):

Higher rate

You must be 'physically disabled' and 'unable to walk' or 'virtually unable to walk'. You can also get it if you are 'severely mentally impaired', have 'severe behavioural problems' and also qualify for the highest care component. Other ways to qualify are that the exertion involved in walking could endanger your health, or if you have had both legs amputated or you are both deaf and blind and need accompanying outdoors.

Lower rate

You must need guidance or supervision from another person most of the time in places that they are unfamiliar walking in. People with visual impairments or chronic anxiety problems can often qualify for this.

Children

As well as meeting the usual rules of entitlement children under 16 must also show that they have substantially more needs than other children in normal health. Quality and quantity of care are important. Children under 16 cannot use the cooking test to receive the lower rate care component.

Publicly funded accommodation

If you live in certain types of publicly funded accommodation, it may affect your Disability Living Allowance. See the sections in Chapter Thirty-seven (Community Care Services).

What the words mean

The meaning of the key phrases in the legislation have been considered on appeal by the Social Security and Child Support Commissioners and by the Courts. The following list explains those meanings and shows that entitlement is not limited to just the clearest or profound disabilities.

Requires

The attention must be 'reasonably required', as distinct from 'medically required', lower threshold which includes social requirements. This also means that you can live alone and/or not receive help you need.

Frequent

Several times, not once nor twice.

Attention

Service of an active nature. Attention implies some physical or personal contact. Attention can also be provided by the spoken word, for example prompting someone to dress or take education. Giving guidance with walking and reading also counts. Attention given by telephone does not count. Can include immediately clearing up after an incident.

Throughout the day

In the middle as well as at the beginning and end of the day.

Bodily functions

Everything to do with how the body works and what it does. It includes breathing, hearing, seeing, reading, eating, drinking, walking, climbing stairs, sleeping, getting in and out of bed, dressing, undressing, washing, cutting up food, shaving, toileting, but does not include cooking, gardening, running errands, shopping or housework.

Continual supervision

Does not mean non-stop (i.e. continuous). The supervision can be precautionary or anticipatory. It does not always have to be active.

Substantial danger

The danger to the person or another must arise from the person's condition and must not be too remote a possibility.

Physically disabled

For mobility component, this includes Down's Syndrome and other mental impairments with a physical cause.

Prolonged

At least 20 minutes.

Repeated

More than once.

Significant portion

At least one hour a day which may consist of one period or a number of different periods. Should be interpreted broadly and considered from the point of view of the attender.

A cooked meal

A main meal, not a snack, prepared and cooked from basic ingredients and using a conventional cooker (e.g. a Spanish omelette, not a cheese omelette). A broad view of claimant's inability should be taken and can include periods when they can cook.

Severely mentally impaired

A state of arrested or incomplete development of mind which includes severe impairment of intelligence and social functioning and which arises before the age of 30.

Severe behavioural problems

Behaviour which is extreme and regularly needs someone else to intervene and physically restrain them in order to prevent injury or damage to property and the behaviour is so unpredictable that another person needs to be present and watching over whenever the person is awake.

Guidance
Leading or supervising or directing – by use of physical contact, signs or the spoken word.

Supervision
Being with the person and at least monitoring the person or circumstances for signs of a need to intervene.

Unable or virtually unable to walk
There is no precise meaning but it includes how fast someone is unable (not unwilling) to walk, how far, how long for and the way they walk, without 'severe discomfort'. For the lower rate lower mobility component, you should give some evidence that guidance or supervision would allow the claimant to overcome an inability to walk out of doors.

How to claim

Claims need to be made as soon as entitlement arises because backdating is almost impossible. If you receive one component, a revision can be requested, (in writing, setting out the reasons and evidence), to include the other component or to change the rate being paid. If your condition changes, a supersession can be requested. However, be aware that a request to revise or supersede potentially opens up the whole claim again, so you could lose the rate or component already awarded, particularly if entitlement is marginal. Seek advice in such cases.

People whose disability arises after the age of 65 are not entitled to Disability Living Allowance (DLA) and should claim Attendance Allowance (AA).

Ring 0800 882200 to request a claim pack - the date of claim will be the date of the phone call, as long as the claim pack is normally returned within six weeks, or complete the tear-off slip in leaflet DLA1, or download and complete the claim form from the DWP website. There is a special claim pack for children.

Terminal illness

There are special rules for people who have a terminal illness. These are that a doctor confirms in writing (on form DS 1500) that the person has a progressive disease and as a consequence they can reasonably be expected not to live for more than six months. Payment continues after the six month period.

A claim can be made by someone acting on your behalf if you are terminally ill (and can be done anonymously if appropriate). The higher rate care component is awarded automatically in terminal illness cases and the mobility component can also be awarded if the mobility questions in the claim pack are completed.

Important points

- the Rightsnet website (www.rightsnet.org.uk) has examples of claim forms and help with completing them. Look under the resources section

- ensure claim forms are filled in comprehensively. The questions can seem repetitive or very obvious, but don't make assumptions - spell out each time what your care or mobility needs are. The decision making process is largely based on the self-assessment in the claim form, so it is vital to get this right from the start; a large number of DLA and AA claims are refused or awarded too low a rate because forms are incorrectly completed

- people can under-estimate or understate the extent of their need for care or supervision or they may over-estimate their walking ability. This is a particular issue when people fill in the claim forms unaided. No one likes to admit that they cannot toilet themselves or feed themselves and this is especially true if people fear hospitalisation or losing their independence if they admit to the extent of help they need

- when describing disability or health conditions, be specific about the effects and consequences of these and don't rely on clinical descriptions or labels (this is particularly so for mental health). Don't assume that DWP staff know what effect someone's medical condition will have on their behaviour, abilities, needs, etc. If someone has a psychotic illness for example, say what effect this has on his or her day to day life

- if you help complete a claim form, use the questions in the claim form to prompt wider questions in order to elicit helpful evidence

- fluctuating conditions and care needs can cause difficulty in establishing entitlement. The rule is that the pattern of needs over a reasonable time should be considered – don't just describe someone on their better days

- confirmation of the condition is required on the form and should be completed by someone who knows them. Ideally, the GP or another professional (for example, social worker, physiotherapist, special needs teacher or community nurse) should sign. NHS GPs are not allowed to charge for this, but some GPs are still reluctant to sign or not charge, particularly as they are no longer required to sign all DLA claim forms. Ask if anyone else in the practice who would be suitable, a practice nurse for example, could sign instead

- it can be helpful to brief people providing supporting evidence and to enclose supporting written evidence with a claim – especially in borderline cases

- entitlement to DLA care component and AA is based on the help or supervision which is needed. Not what is actually received. The help and/or care need not be provided by a paid person, nor by a relative. It can also be provided by a combination of different people

- DLA and AA are paid irrespective of income and capital and whether or not someone is in work, training or education. Entry to work should not be used by the DWP as a reason to reconsider entitlement. However, starting work may be interpreted by the DWP as being a relevant change of circumstances, thus triggering further enquiries

- DLA and AA do not have to be spent on disability related expenditure (though AA and the care component of DLA, but not the mobility component, may be counted as income by local authorities assessing charges for community care services)

- the qualifying conditions for both AA and DLA are very geared to physical disability and can be difficult to claim if you have a mental health problem or learning disability to claim. They may need additional supporting evidence

- some groups can face greater difficulty in making a clear cut case for DLA or AA. These include people who have a sensory impairment, people whose first language is not English or who have particular cultural concepts of disability, children with behavioural or mental health problems and people with confusional conditions

- there is no element of AA for mobility, but if someone needs frequent help each day with walking or being guided, this can count as satisfying the need for frequent attention during the day. This also will help make the case for DLA middle or higher rate care components

- people who ask for a revision, supersession or appeal on negative decisions may need supporting evidence from health or care professionals. Many claimants will be on low incomes and unable to pay for medical reports privately

- there appears to be significant scope for increasing take up of DLA/AA among children with a disability and adults with mental health problems or who are deaf

- if you are a child under 16, the payment of DLA will be made to your parent or guardian. At age 16 the possibility of the child themselves receiving it should be considered by the DWP but payment to parents can continue beyond this, even inappropriately and undermining a young person's independence (see page 11 for information about payments).

- help needed with housework or gardening does not count as personal care but may be an indication of personal care needs and act as a prompt for an adviser to ask questions when helping complete a claim form

- awards are often short-term and subject to renewal. This can mean having to complete forms periodically and supplying further medical and other evidence

- the GP/Consultant may be contacted by the Disability Benefits Centre to supply additional evidence on a factual report. The questions may vary according to the person's condition. Doctors should normally provide such evidence for claims as this is required under their NHS contract

- awards of DLA and AA can trigger entitlement to other benefits and tax credits or higher amounts

- if DWP arranges for an Examining Medical Practitioner (EMP) to visit (usually after a new claim) the adviser should try to be present if they can. Or at least brief the person being visited about what to expect. Some EMPs have a reputation for being unfriendly or too rushed. If benefit is refused because of the EMP's report, you can ask for a copy of it. Don't be afraid to challenge an EMP report - it is often based on no more than a 30 minute interview and may even include factual inaccuracies as well as misinterpretations. At Tribunal, you may need counter-evidence from another doctor to show that the EMP was wrong or mistaken

- EMPs are employed by Atos Origin who have a contract with the DWP to provide medical assessment services for benefits.

However, complaints should be dealt with by the DWP and responsibility for dealing with complaints should not be passed over to their contractor

- the DWP have a process of Periodic Enquiries directed at people receiving DLA. This may include a postal questionnaire, home visit or a medical examination. See bullet points above and seek advice.

Attendance Allowance (AA)

Who is entitled?

You:

- must be aged 65 or older
- must show you need help with bodily functions and/or supervision to avoid danger to self or others. The rules of entitlement are the same as the higher and middle care component of DLA
- must have needed help/supervision for at least 6 months (note: this is different to DLA).

How to claim

Claim on form DS2, from social security or Jobcentre Plus offices, or telephone 0800 882200 which will issue and date stamp a claim form. These should be returned within six weeks. Or download and complete a claim form from the DWP website.

Important issues

See above section on DLA.

Chapter Four: Benefits for people who are unable to work because of disability or ill health

If you have an illness or disability which means that you are unable to work ('incapable of work') you should be able to receive one or more of the benefits described in this chapter. Which benefit you receive will normally depend upon whether you are employed, have paid National Insurance contributions or fulfil certain other conditions. You may also be able to receive Income Support and other means-tested benefits, either to top-up these benefits, or as an alternative source of income if you don't meet the conditions of entitlement (particularly if you have not paid enough National Insurance contributions).

The main benefits are:

- Statutory Sick Pay (SSP)
- Incapacity Benefit (IB)
- Severe Disablement Allowance (SDA).

Statutory Sick Pay (SSP)

This is a social security benefit, which is paid by employers, for a maximum of 28 weeks to employees who are too ill to work. It is not means-tested and counts as income for means-tested benefits. It is not paid for the first three days of any period of absence (unless the person has been on SSP within the last eight weeks). It may be paid in addition to any occupational sick pay scheme that an employer has (people sometimes confuse the two). Occupational sick pay may last for more than 28 weeks when SSP stops. Some employers (usually with less than about 100 employees) may reclaim their spending on SSP from the Inland Revenue.

Who is entitled?

To qualify for SSP you must:

- be under 65 when the period of sickness begins
- have average gross earnings more than the lower earnings limit for National Insurance (currently £79 pw)
- be incapable of work
- have been incapable of work for at least 4 days (unless they have been ill within the previous 8 weeks)
- be within a period of entitlement
- have notified the employer.

SSP is only paid for days that you normally work on ('qualifying days'). There are special rules where normal working patterns vary and advice may be needed.

Who is an employee?

Attempts by some employers to circumvent employees' rights by classing them as self-employed or as sub-contractors may be challengeable and specialist employment law advice should be sought in such cases.

There are no minimum hours of work needed to qualify for SSP and it is possible to receive SSP from more than one employer (for example, if someone has two part-time jobs). It is also possible to be unfit for one employment but fit for another and so receive both SSP and earnings from the other job.

Notification

Notification of sickness should be made in a manner agreed with your employer and as soon as possible.

For the first seven days of sickness you self-certify your sickness. After that, a medical certificate (Med 3, or a Med 5 if it is retrospective) should be provided. Medical evidence for SSP and Incapacity Benefit can also be provided by people other than a doctor – for example, a community nurse, physiotherapist or social worker, if it is reasonable in the circumstances (e.g. if you are unable to obtain access to a GP's services). Additional evidence from other professionals may also help in borderline or unusual situations.

An employer who dismisses an employee solely or mainly to avoid paying SSP remains liable for paying SSP during the period of entitlement, or until the contract of employment, was due to end. It may also be unfair dismissal and/or discrimination and the person should be advised to consult an expert in employment law.

Disputes about Statutory Sick Pay

If your employer refuses to pay you SSP, you have the right to ask your employer to explain why. If you disagree with their explanation or if they fail to provide information within a reasonable time, you can then ask the local Inland Revenue Contributions Office to decide what you are entitled to. You must ask the Inland Revenue to decide matters within six months of when you think you should have received SSP.

If you are dismissed for enforcing your right to SSP, you will not be able to take action for unfair dismissal unless you have worked for the employer for at least a year.

After 28 weeks SSP, the employer is legally required to send you a notice (SSP1) telling them that they have had the maximum amount of SSP. You then complete the SSP1 and send it to

Jobcentre Plus who will use it to award Incapacity Benefit, linking to any time on SSP. The form must also be sent if you are not entitled to SSP for other reasons so that you can use it to claim Incapacity Benefit

This is paid by the DWP to people who have enough National Insurance contributions (unless they qualify under the special rules for young people). Contributions paid by both employed and self-employed people count, as do some National Insurance credits.

Incapacity Benefit

Incapacity Benefit is payable if you:

- have paid or been credited with enough National Insurance Contributions

- are accepted as being incapable of work.

Some people aged between 16 and 25 may be able to receive Incapacity Benefit even if they don't have enough National Insurance contributions and even if they are still in full time education.

There are three rates of Incapacity Benefit:

Short-term Incapacity Benefit at the lower rate

This is the equivalent of the old Sickness Benefit and is paid for the first 28 weeks' incapacity to people who don't qualify for Statutory Sick Pay (SSP) from an employer. It is tax-free.

Short-term Incapacity Benefit at the higher rate

This is paid from 29-52 weeks' incapacity to people who have either received the lower rate, or SSP (or a combination of these). It is taxable.

Long-term Incapacity Benefit

This is the equivalent of the old Invalidity Benefit and is paid from 53 weeks incapacity onwards to people who have received the short-term higher rate, or from 29 weeks to people receiving the higher care component of Disability Living Allowance (DLA) or who are terminally ill. This is taxable.

The following additions can be paid with the basic benefit:

- Age allowances (paid with long term rate only)
- there are two age additions, depending on the age at which your incapacity for work began:
- incapacity began before age 35: higher age allowance (£15.55)
- incapacity began between 35-45: lower age allowance (£7.80)
- some people who were on Invalidity Benefit before it was abolished on 13 April 1995, may receive a different age allowance.

Young people

If you are aged over 16 but under 20, you may receive Incapacity Benefit without National Insurance contributions, provided that your incapacity began before your 20th birthday and if you have also been incapable of working continually for at least 28 weeks.

If you are aged from 20 up to 25, you can qualify for Incapacity Benefit without contributions if you have been incapable of work for at least 28 weeks and:

- you were on an education or training course for at least three months before you were 20
- you have left that course

- the course ended within the previous two tax years before the calendar year (e.g. for January 2004 to January 2005, the course must have ended between April 2001 and April 2003)
- you claim before your 25th birthday.

Adult dependants

An addition for an adult dependant may only be paid if your spouse is aged over 60 or they care for children.

If you are entitled to one of the short-term rates, or are claiming for a dependant you don't live with but whom you maintain financially, the dependency addition is not paid if the dependant's net earnings are greater than the amount of the addition. When the dependant is living with someone receiving the long-term rate it is not paid if their net earnings are more than £55.65 a week.

Child dependants

If you claimed Incapacity Benefit or Severe Disablement Allowance before 7 April 2003 and qualify for a child dependency addition, you will continue to receive it until this element is eventually transferred to Child Tax Credit. New child dependency additions will be included in Child Tax Credit.

How to claim

Claim using the Incapacity Benefit claim pack (SC1) available from local Jobcentre Plus offices. A medical certificate is not required for the first seven days of incapacity, after which a medical certificate (Med 3 or Med 5 as appropriate or other evidence) must be sent to the office handling the claim.

If you work for an employer and do not get SSP, or have come to the end of your SSP (or you leave work), you should complete and send in the SSP1 claim pack which you employer must send to you.

Claims can be backdated for up to three months provided that evidence (e.g. a Med 5) is produced and the conditions of entitlement are met.

If you claim Incapacity Benefit and you live in a Jobcentre Plus area, you will be asked to attend a Work Focused Interview to discuss employment possibilities. (See Chapter 18 for further information).

Incapacity for work – what it means

Incapacity for work is decided according to legislation and there are two tests of incapacity, the Own Occupation Test and the Personal Capability Assessment.

The Own Occupation Test

Are you incapable of doing the work which you were normally employed to do before falling sick?

The own occupation test applies for the first 28 weeks of the claim provided that you have been undertaking paid work of 16 hours or more a week for more than eight weeks in the 21 weeks before the date of claim. If you have not worked for this period (for example, you are unemployed and receiving Jobseeker's Allowance), then the Personal Capability Assessment test will apply from the start of your claim.

The Personal Capability Assessment (PCA)

The PCA is an assessment of someone's ability to perform a range of work related activities. The test is objective - actual ability to do real jobs is not considered and non-medical factors such as age, qualifications, education and past work experience are not relevant. It is often based on an examination and questioning by a doctor employed by the DWP, usually after ten weeks incapacity.

The PCA is divided into a physical assessment and a mental assessment.

For each assessment there is a list of descriptors. These are statements describing the level of disability and you are asked to rate your ability against the descriptors. Points are then allocated to the different descriptors. Incapacity for work is then decided on the number of points scored. (See Further Information and Guidance Section for all the descriptors).

To be treated as incapable of work, you must score a total of either:

- 15 points from the physical abilities list or
- 10 points from the mental abilities list or
- 15 points if you have a combination of physical and mental incapacity.

If you have a combination of mental and physical abilities and you score between six and nine (inclusive) in the mental disability list, then a score of nine is added to the physical test. Scores of less than six are ignored.

In the physical abilities list you can only be awarded points for either walking or using stairs - not both: the highest score that you qualify for is awarded. For all other activities in the physical test, the highest score for each descriptor is awarded.

For the mental test you are awarded points for each of the descriptors which apply. This means that up to nine points may be awarded for each activity.

The PCA acts as the gateway to benefit. In addition, if you attend a medical examination as part of the assessment you may be asked for additional information about what you can do in spite of your illness or disability. This information forms a Capability Report which may be used to give advice and support to help you get back to work.

More about the rules of entitlement

When the own occupation test applies, you should send in medical certificates (Med 3) from your doctor.

When the PCA applies, benefit continues to be paid whilst the PCA is being undertaken. Med 3 certificates should continue to be supplied until Jobcentre Plus notifies you otherwise. Med 5 certificates are for retrospective evidence.

If the Med 3 has identified a condition which may result in exemption (including mental health problems or a learning disability), Jobcentre Plus will contact your doctor to enquire about the severity of these, and this could exempt you from the assessment. If exempt, Jobcentre Plus will notify both you and your doctor. No further medical certificates need be supplied and you don't have to undertake the PCA.

Everyone who is not exempt is sent a questionnaire (IB 50) to complete which forms part of the PCA. This asks questions about your physical limitations in the functional areas (although a small section of the form also asks about anxiety, depression and other mental health problems).

Failure to return the IB 50 without good cause may result in you being found capable of work and your benefit is then stopped (Jobcentre Plus should send reminders before doing this).

Following the return of the IB 50, the Decision Maker at Jobcentre Plus will decide whether there is a need for a medical examination. Everyone with a mental health issue will be referred for a medical examination (unless they fall into an exemption category).

With mental health assessments, the DWP's doctor must be satisfied that the effects arise from a diagnosed psychiatric problem. If the condition is undiagnosed, the test will be applied and if it confirms a mental health problem, further information will be sought from your own doctor (which could be either your GP or a consultant).

The DWP's doctor then sends a report to the decision maker with advice on incapacity. Decisions about Incapacity Benefit entitlement are always made by DWP decision makers.

Exemptions

Some people are accepted as being incapable of work and do not have to undergo the PCA. It is important to check whether or not you could be exempted from the PCA. The following are exempt:

You can be treated as incapable of work for any day you are:

- a hospital in-patient
- under observation because of contact with, or suspicion of being a carrier of, an infectious or contagious disease and have been excluded from work by a certificate of a Medical Officer for Environmental Health
- receiving particular treatment, e.g. radiotherapy, chemotherapy, weekly renal dialysis
- pregnant, where there is a risk to health or safety of the mother or baby, or for a period 6 weeks before and 2 weeks after the birth
- terminally ill (death can be reasonably expected within six months)
- receiving the higher rate care component of Disability Living Allowance
- accepted as 80% disabled for the purposes of Severe Disablement Allowance or Industrial Disablement Benefit
- registered as blind.

Also, people with one of the following medical conditions:

- dementia
- tetraplegia
- persistent vegetative state
- paraplegia or uncontrolled involuntary movements or ataxia which effectively make the claimant paraplegic.

Or, where there is medical evidence that the person has one of the following conditions:

- severe learning difficulties (defined as 'arrested or incomplete physical development of the brain, or severe damage to the brain, which involves severe impairment of intelligence and social functioning')
- 'a severe mental illness involving the presence of mental disease, which severely and adversely affects a person's mood or behaviour, and which severely restricts his social functioning, or his awareness of his immediate environment'
- a severe and progressive neurological or muscle wasting disease
- an active and progressive form of inflammatory polyarthritis
- a progressive impairment of cardio-respiratory function which severely and persistently limits effort tolerance
- dense paralysis of upper limb, trunk and lower limb on one side
- multiple effects of impairment of function of the brain or nervous system causing severe and irreversible motor, sensory and intellectual deficits
- manifestations of severe and progressive immune deficiency

states characterised by severe constitutional disease or opportunistic infections or tumour formation (e.g. AIDS).

If a certificate of exemption is issued, you and your doctor will be notified and you will not have to provide medical certificates unless the claim is reviewed.

Important points

- people who fail the PCA may need further medical evidence to support their incapacity for work claim. GPs and others can continue to provide medical certificates (and other evidence) in support of this

- people with a mental illness or learning disability may fail to return the IB50 as they don't feel it is relevant to them. They will need support or encouragement to understand the relevance and importance of this form and it is important that doctors give detailed information about the severity of the person's condition

- when completing an IB 50 it may be useful to refer to the PCA indicators (see page 299) of the Further information and guidance section

- if your Incapacity Benefit is stopped because you have not passed the PCA, seek, advice and support with submitting an appeal and with making a new claim for Incapacity Benefit (as the new claim should be decided afresh in the light of current evidence)

- there is a very high success rate in appeals against refusals of Incapacity Benefit, including cases where people have appealed when cut off after receiving Incapacity Benefit. As well as considering matters such as whether or not enough points have been awarded in the PCA, appeals can also consider whether or not a full and proper medical examination took place, whether or not the PCA was legally valid and whether or not the original award of Incapacity Benefit has been properly superseded

- if you have appealed, you may claim Income Support (but if claimed on these grounds, it is paid at a lower rate and there are no National Insurance credits). You may also claim Jobseeker's Allowance without prejudicing your appeal

- a large number of disputes about incapacity for work arise because poor quality information has been presented to the DWP or because the full implications of someone's condition have not been put across. This can include poor quality reports by doctors contracted to work for the DWP

- there have been many public concerns about the quality of work by the doctors contracted to the DWP and so it is prudent not to rely on their findings alone

- while Incapacity Benefit is not means-tested, if someone has an occupational or personal pension and claims Incapacity Benefit after 6 April 2001, half of the pension above £85 a week is deducted from their Incapacity Benefit. So if someone has an occupational pension of £100 a week, their Incapacity Benefit will be reduced by £7.50

- if you have given up work on health grounds after being paid by your employer whilst off sick, and your ex-employer then pays you a pension, you may not have claimed Incapacity Benefit. You should claim it as soon as you can, as it is paid in addition to the pension (but see above for effect on the amount paid)

- people of retirement age (65 for men, 60 for women), can't receive the long-term rate of Incapacity Benefit but the additional amount paid to people who received Incapacity Benefit benefit before the age of 45 (known as the 'age addition' may continue

- many people on Incapacity Benefit can find that they have an income just above Income Support level. It is important to check if you could be lifted onto Income Support through qualification to additional premiums such as those for carers and severe disability. It is also worth exploring help with NHS costs and discretionary Housing Benefit payments for people who are not on Income Support

- people on Incapacity Benefit can have a break off of up to eight weeks (i.e. benefit weeks: Sunday to Saturday) and return to the benefit. For others, it may be possible for people to have breaks of either 52 weeks or two years in work, but seek advice on this, preferably before someone starts work

- people making new Incapacity Benefit claims and who are not in paid work are increasingly being asked to have Work Focused Interviews (see Chapter 18). This type of intervention can be expected to increase. In cases when such an interview is not appropriate, representations can be made for it to be waived.

- If Jobcentre Plus are uncertain about your continuing incapacity for work, they may ask you to undergo a medical examination. Sometimes this can be triggered by undertaking voluntary or part-time work.

- A finding at a medical examination may not be, by itself, a legal ground for ending Incapacity Benefit.

- In some areas, the Pathways to Work pilot schemes are opertating which involve work focussed interviews on a regular basis, access to a Jobcentre Plus Adviser Discretionary Fund for work and training related costs, a Return to Work Credit and additional rehabilitation services. These areas are: Derbyshire, Renfrewshire, Inverclyde, Argyll, Bute, Brigend, Rhondda Cynon Taff, East Lancashire, Essex, Gateshead, South Tyneside and Somerset. (See Chapter 21)

Working while on Incapacity Benefit

You can continue to be treated as incapable of work and continue to receive Incapacity Benefit, Severe Disablement Allowance and/or Income Support on the grounds of incapacity for work, if you do work which is:

- voluntary work
- permitted work
- an approved, unpaid work trial agreed in writing by Jobcentre Plus, or
- work as a councillor or as a disability member of a Tribunal.

Voluntary work

A volunteer is someone who is: 'involved in voluntary work, other than for a close relative, where the only payment received by him or due to be paid to him... is in respect of any expenses reasonably incurred in connection with that work.'

A close relative is defined as: 'a parent, parent-in-law, son, son-in-law, daughter, daughter-in-law, step-parent, step-son, step-daughter, brother, sister or spouse of any of the preceding persons, or if that person is one of a couple, the other member of that couple.'

Government policy is to encourage such voluntary work because it promotes people's health and well-being and may be a route back into employment. However, many people receiving Incapacity Benefit may be anxious that voluntary work will jeopardise their benefit and experience shows that Jobcentre Plus staff may not fully understand this point or be inclined to question peoples' incapacity. It is therefore useful to tell Jobcentre Plus about the details of any voluntary work being done and your limitations, preferably before it starts.

Permitted work

To count as permitted work, the work must be for less than 16 hours week and:

- pay, on average, no more than £72 a week in a 26 week period. This period can be extended for another 26 weeks if a Job Broker, Jobcentre Plus Personal Adviser or Disability Employment Adviser agrees it will help you towards sustaining paid work of 16 or more hours a week

- after that 26/52 week period, the permitted work must pay no more than £20 per week
- be in supported permitted work, which pays no more than £72 a week. There is no time limit on this work. This kind of arrangement is more suitable for someone who is not realistically capable of moving back into full-time work for the foreseeable future.

Supported permitted work must be done with ongoing support or supervision from a professional caseworker (from a voluntary or public sector body, including nursing staff, social workers, support workers or Connexions/careers advisers). It includes work done under medical supervision in hospital as well as work in sheltered workshops and, more importantly, work in an ordinary paid job.

It is important to notify Jobcentre Plus (in writing) about any work and to explain why it should be treated as permitted work or supported permitted work.

If you also receive means-tested benefits such as Income Support or Housing/Council Tax Benefits you are still bound by the lower earnings limits for these benefits (£20). This lack of symmetry in the social security rules undermines the good intentions behind the permitted work rules and means that most people thinking of doing permitted work will need advice and help to work out the effect on their overall income and benefit and tax credit entitlement before they start work. Permitted work allowances increase with the National Minimum Wage (usually October).

Severe Disablement Allowance

This non-contributory benefit was abolished in April 2001 but people who were already receiving it before the 6 April 2001 may continue to receive it.

Chapter Five: Benefits for work related accidents and illness

What are they?

There are a number of benefits for people whose ill health or disability is related to their employment. These are:

- Disablement Benefit
- Reduced Earnings Allowance
- Retirement Allowance.

They are often called industrial injury benefits and they are paid to if you have a disability or health problem which results from an accident at work or from a prescribed industrial disease. They are non-taxable, and non-contributory and they can be paid whether or not you are working and regardless of your income or capital. They are also paid without having to prove negligence by the employer or if the employee had been negligent themselves and whether or not you received compensation.

For all industrial injury benefits you must be able to show that they meet the industrial injury condition. This is that you:

- were an employed earner (i.e. not self employed) and either
- had an accident arising out of and in the course of your employment or
- suffer from a prescribed industrial disease and
- as a result of that accident or disease you have a loss of faculty and because of that loss of faculty, you are disabled.

Disablement Benefit

Who is entitled?

You must:

- meet the conditions mentioned above and as a result, have a disablement which is assessed as being at least 14%
- had the accident or contracted the prescribed disease at least 90 days ago (excluding Sundays).

The amount of benefit depends on the percentage assessment of your disability (a minimum of 14% is required).

It is possible to get a higher rate of Disablement Benefit by also qualifying for Constant Attendance Allowance (this is not the same as Attendance Allowance; it is a benefit specifically for work related disability) or Exceptionally Severe Disablement Allowance (also a specific industrial injuries benefit).

Constant Attendance Allowance

You must be entitled to Disablement Benefit based on a 100% disability assessment and also need constant attendance as a result. As with Attendance Allowance, this can trigger higher rates of means-tested benefits and is ignored as income for all benefits.

Exceptionally Severe Disablement Allowance

Paid if you are entitled to one of the two higher rates of Constant Attendance Allowance and are likely to remain so permanently.

Reduced Earnings Allowance (REA)

REA is only payable if you had an accident or started to suffer from a disease before 1 October 1990. A successful first claim can still be made now if this can be demonstrated, although payment is not backdated for more than three months.

REA can compensate people under pension age who have had at least a 1% disability assessment, who are in work and who are unable to follow their regular occupation or to do work of an equivalent standard.

People over pension age are only entitled to REA if they remain in regular employment after retirement.

The amount of benefit paid depends on current earnings and the difference from previous earnings.

Retirement Allowance

Retirement Allowance is a reduced rate of REA for people over retirement age who have given up regular employment, and who previously qualified for REA of at least £2 a week.

How to claim

Claim forms are available from Jobcentre Plus local offices. As with all benefits it is best not to delay making a claim. The first trigger for a claim is 16 weeks after the accident or contracting a prescribed disease.

A claim for Constant Attendance Allowance can be treated as a claim for Attendance Allowance or Disability Living Allowance. However, this should not be relied on and some people will be better off claiming Attendance Allowance or Disability Living Allowance. It is important to get advice on this point.

Important points

- people who are on government supported training schemes and who are not employees, are not covered by these benefits. However, in England the Department for Education and Skills runs the Analogous Industrial Injuries Scheme which provides identical help to trainees. Tel 0800 590 395. There are similar schemes in Scotland, Wales and Northern Ireland

- people whose condition has deteriorated since their award was made can ask for an 'unforeseen aggravation' review. Medical evidence may be needed to support an increased award

- in law, the definition of 'accident' is very broad. It includes things such as malicious noise, conversations and the harmful behaviour of others – which may have led to your disability or illness

- it is often worth claiming one of these benefits even if your condition isn't severe enough to qualify – if you deteriorate later the claim can be renewed

- if you have had an accident at work it is important to register this with Jobcentre Plus in order to protect a possible future claim. You should also record it in your employer's accident or risk reporting system. However, failure to do so is not fatal to a successful claim

- if you are trying to prove you had an accident that happened some time ago, your doctor may be asked to supply evidence that they were consulted at the time

- the percentage assessment takes account of someone's abilities and mental and physical health compared to what would be normal for someone of the same age and gender

- the assessment will be reduced for any disability or ill health which is not employment related

- prescribed industrial diseases are set out in legislation. They include particular diseases and also occupations in which one must contract the disease. A full list is contained in the Child Poverty Action Group's Welfare Benefits and Tax Credits Handbook

- accidents which are not work-related won't qualify. However, accidents while travelling to and from work may qualify depending on the circumstances

- you may still qualify if you were breaking work rules at the time, or even if what you were doing was reasonably incidental to your work. People who have been injured because of someone else's actions (even if they were skylarking or had no ill-interest) may count as accidents caused by natural events. It is best to give the benefit of the doubt in these matters and make a claim

- Disability Living Allowance care component or Attendance Allowance (AA/DLA) will be reduced by the amount of Constant Attendance Allowance being paid. Constant Attendance Allowance rates vary according to the extent of disability and may be higher than the rates of AA/DLA, so may be worth claiming, even if AA/DLA is being paid

- if someone dies as a result of an industrial accident or a prescribed industrial disease, their married partner will normally be entitled to a Bereavement Payment without having to meet the normal National Insurance Contribution rules

- people who receive compensation for an accident will have the amount of damages they receive repaid to the DWP to take account of benefits they have received for the accident. It may be possible to include the reduction as part of the damages claim – seek legal advice.

This is a complex area and specialist advice should be sought. Solicitors specialising in personal injury matters may overlook social security entitlement.

Chapter Six: War Pensions

What are they?

War Pensions are non-contributory, non-means tested benefits for people who have a disability or ill health which is connected with service (including National Service) in the UK's Armed Forces. This includes service in the Home Guard, the Auxiliary Services, Reserves or Cadets. Civilians are also included for physical injuries acquired during the Second World War or during merchant naval service in certain military conflicts. They can be paid whether or not people are in work and are tax-free. The first £10 of any War Pension is ignored as income for means-tested benefits and all but three local authorities ignore them as income for Housing and Council Tax Benefits.

The Government plans to replace War Pensions with a new armed forces pension and compensation scheme from April 2005.

War Pensions are administered by the Veterans Agency (part of the Ministry of Defence).

They are not the same as a forces pension, paid to someone who has built up an occupational pension whilst serving in the Armed Forces in the same way that any other employee in an occupational pension scheme builds up a pension.

War Pensions consist of the following benefits:

- War Disablement Pension.

Plus the following additional (supplementary) allowances on top:

- Mobility Supplement
- Constant Attendance Allowance

- Unemployability Supplement
- Allowance for Lowered Standard of Occupation
- Clothing Allowance
- Treatment Allowance
- Exceptionally Severe Disablement Allowance
- Severe Disablement Occupational Allowance.

Who is entitled?

People whose health or disability was caused by or made worse by service in the armed forces. There is no list of qualifying conditions and both physical and mental (e.g. post-traumatic stress disorder) conditions are included. Also, conditions with uncertain causes (such as multiple sclerosis, diabetes or motor neurone disease) are included if they arose while on service. Conditions need not be caused by hostile activity, and conditions caused by participation in leisure activities (e.g. a disability caused by playing in a regimental rugby team) will also count.

The amount of War Disablement Pension depends on the percentage assessed disability. If it is less than 20%, a lump sum is paid. Like industrial injuries benefits, it is possible to have these assessment decision reviewed if the condition changes (as it may do with age).

Mobility Supplement

Unlike Disability Living Allowance mobility component there is no upper age limit for this. You must be assessed as having a 40% disability and they must be unable or virtually unable to walk. You cannot receive both the Mobility Supplement and Disability Living Allowance mobility component.

Constant Attendance Allowance

This is for people with at least an 80% assessed disability who also need personal care, attention or supervision. There are four rates and the three highest rates are more than Attendance Allowance and Disability Living Allowance care component. You cannot receive both the Constant Attendance Allowance and Attendance Allowance or Disability Living Allowance.

Unemployability Supplement

This is for people with at least a 60% assessed disability and who are permanently unable to work.

Allowance for Lowered Standard of Occupation

This is for people with at least a 40% assessed disability who are unable to follow their normal occupation or work which is equivalent.

Clothing Allowance

This is a small annual allowance if the qualifying disability causes exceptional wear and tear on clothes.

Treatment Allowance

This tops up the War Disablement Pension if a person loses earnings because they receive medical treatment.

Exceptionally Severe Disablement Allowance

This is an additional payment for people receiving one of the two highest rates of Constant Attendance allowance.

Severe Disablement Occupational Allowance

This is for people receiving one of the two highest rates of Constant Attendance Allowance whom are in work.

Comforts Allowance

This is for people receiving the Unemployability Supplement or Constant Attendance Allowance.

Age Allowance

This is an additional allowance paid to people over 65 who have at least a 40% assessed disability.

War Widows Pensions

These are for widows or widowers whose death was caused by or substantially hastened by a qualifying illness or disability. Sometimes, a pension can be paid to other dependants.

How to claim

A claim is made by obtaining a claim form from the Veterans Agency on 0800 169 2277, or by writing to them.

A claim should be made as soon as possible (it is easier if it is within seven years of leaving the Armed Forces). Backdating of payment for up to three years is possible in some circumstances. However, for civilians a claim must be made within three months of the injury.

If a War Disablement Pension is awarded, the Exceptionally Severe Disablement Allowance, Severe Disablement Occupational Allowance, Comforts Allowance and Age Allowances are paid automatically. All the other additional benefits should be specifically claimed.

There is a system of reviews and appeals which is separate from the main social security system and specialist help should be sought.

Important points

- many older people miss out on claiming war pensions (for example for conditions caused while on National Service). Injuries caused in youth may worsen with age or you may have not had sufficient help and support on discharge from the forces

- there are additional discretionary payments for a range of matters, such as hospital treatment costs, chiropody, appliances, adaptations to the home, residential and nursing home fees, respite care and funeral costs. Seek advice in each case

- former Far East prisoners of war or their widows or widowers are entitled to a tax free lump sum of £10,000.

Chapter Seven: Carer's Allowance (CA)

Carer's Allowance (CA) is a non-contributory benefit for people who spend time looking after someone who receives the middle or higher rate of Disability Living Allowance (DLA) care component or who receives Attendance Allowance (AA). It is taxable and counts as income for means-tested benefits, but entitlement to Carer's Allowance can increase entitlement to means-tested benefits as higher amounts (extra premiums) may become payable. Carer's Allowance used to be known as Invalid Care Allowance until 1 April 2003.

Who is entitled?

You must:

- be aged 16 or over
- care for someone who receives Attendance Allowance or either the middle or the higher rate care component of Disability Living Allowance (or the war pension or industrial injury equivalents)
- earn no more than £79 net a week
- not be in education for 21 or more hours supervised study each week
- regularly and substantially care for the person on AA/DLA for at least 35 hours a week. That doesn't mean 35 hours of active caring however - being around as a precaution and time spent preparing or clearing up after caring can be enough.

How to claim

Claim on form DS700, from local Jobcentre Plus offices or ring 0800 882200. It is best to claim when the person being cared for also claims AA/DLA as it can be awarded retrospectively when or if AA/DLA is awarded. It is also possible to backdate a claim for Carer's Allowance for 3 months if the conditions of entitlement were met.

Important points

- you cannot receive both CA and certain other non means-tested benefits e.g. Incapacity Benefit, Bereavement Benefits or state Retirement Pension. However, it may still be worth making a claim as having underlying entitlement can still create entitlement to higher rates of means-tested benefits (see the point below)

- an award (or underlying entitlement through overlapping benefits) of CA can lead to the inclusion of a Carer's Premium in the calculation of Income Support, Housing/Council Tax Benefit. It is not uncommon for the Carer's Premium to be left out by Jobcentre Plus, especially if entitlement arises under the underlying entitlement rules

- carers aged over 65 used to be excluded from Invalid Care Allowance, but can now receive CA. However, most will have overlapping entitlement to Retirement Pension and so not receive it. But because of the additional means-tested benefits they could receive, it is often still worth claiming and there are many older carers on low incomes who could gain from this measure

- people who claimed Invalid Care Allowance (the old name for CA) before 7 April 2003 and who qualify for a child dependency addition will continue to receive it until this element is eventually transferred to Child Tax Credit. New child dependency additions will be included in Child Tax Credit

- people on CA receive National Insurance credits and if you are under 60 and unemployed, you do not have to sign on

- check the effect on CA when the person being cared for or the carer has a stay in hospital

- respite care in publicly funded residential care means that Attendance Allowance or Disability Living Allowance care component stops after 28 days. This also means that the CA stops, so careful planning is needed to avoid problems and disruption to peoples' income

- if the person being cared for dies, CA can continue for the carer for eight weeks

- people who are carers who are not entitled to CA, may be entitled to Home Responsibilities Protection to help with their Retirement Pension

- as CA is paid for looking after a named individual, it is possible for say a couple both on AA to have two different people getting CA for looking after them. So a couple both on AA/DLA could each receive CA for looking after each other. However, when two or more carers each spend 35 hours a week caring for the same person, only one is entitled to CA. Also, if a carer looks after more than one person for 35 hours a week, they can only receive CA in respect of one of them

- the carer does not need to be related to the person they care for and can also be paid (provided that it is less than the earnings limit)

- if a carer receives CA, it will stop the person being looked after being entitled to the Severe Disability Premium in any means-tested benefits. It is very important to check this before claiming CA and to seek advice

- a claim for CA by someone under 60 will trigger an interview in Jobcentre Plus areas to look at work options.

Chapter Eight: Retirement Pension

What is it and who is entitled?

Retirement Pension (RP) is a contributory benefit paid to people over pension age (60 for women, 65 for men – these ages are to be equalised at 65 for everyone on a phased basis from 2010). RP is taxable but is not affected by earnings, retirement or non-retirement, income or any savings. There are three categories of RP:

- Category A: Paid to people who have enough National Insurance contributions (including credits). A reduced rate of RP may be paid if you have gaps in your contributions

- Category B: Paid to people who don't have enough contributions but who can use their spouse's contributions to qualify (including contributions of a late spouse or former spouse)

- Category D: A flat-rate, non-contributory Retirement Pension paid to people over 80 who don't have enough National Insurance contributions to receive either a Category A or B pension. This will be especially relevant for people who have gaps because of ill-health or disability or who have lived abroad.

How to claim

You can claim up to four months before reaching pension age and you will usually be automatically contacted by the Pension Service to do this, however, Retirement Pension won't be paid automatically so the claim is still necessary. Alternatively, you can get a claim pack by phoning 0845 300 1084. A claim can be backdated for up to three months if a claim is made after pension age. Category D Retirement Pension must be specifically claimed at age 80.

Important points

- a higher rate of RP can be paid if you defer claiming it for five years after pension age. You can also give up your pension in this timescale in order to do the same. However, you should seek advice about whether this is worth doing as the additional rate of RP may be less than the amount of RP you lose by deferring – full five year deferment only increases pension by about 37%. This is expected to change

- Category A and B RP may include additional amounts from Graduated Retirement Benefit, the State Earnings Related Pension Scheme and the State Second Pension. These additions will be automatically calculated by the Pension Service and do not need to be claimed. People who have been on Incapacity Benefit with an age addition will also receive a higher rate

- sometimes you may find that National Insurance credits (e.g. for unemployment, sickness or caring) have not been put on your records or that an employer has failed to make contributions you have actually paid. You should seek advice in such cases

- people receiving RP who are 80 or over receive an age addition of 25 pence a week. This figure has been unchanged for a very long time

- people who claimed Retirement Pension before 7 April 2003 and who qualify for a child dependency addition will continue to receive it until this element is eventually transferred to Child Tax Credit. New child dependency additions will no longer exist and a claim for Child Tax Credit should be made instead

- anyone of any age can receive a forecast of their future RP (and sometimes occupational pension) entitlement by phoning 0845 3000 168

- people who are thinking of moving abroad should seek advice as in many countries their RP will be paid at a frozen level unless they resume residence in the UK or move to a country which has a Reciprocal Agreement with the UK that covers Retirement Pension annual increases

- one-off, annual Winter Fuel Payments of £200 are paid to people aged 60 or over in the week of the third Monday in September. Normally people receiving RP, Pension Credit, Carer's Allowance and some other benefits will not have to do anything to receive this. However, people not on a benefit will have to make a separate claim. People in hospital for more than a year and those on Income Support in care homes for more than 12 weeks, do not qualify. An additional £100 will be paid to people aged 80 or over, on top of the Winter Fuel Payment. People aged 75 or older will receive a one-off £100 payment towards council tax bills in 2004. It will be paid at the same time as the Winter Fuel Payment.

Chapter Nine: Means-tested benefits

What are they?

Means-tested benefits are a very important part of the UK's social security system. They can top up other income or even form all of someone's income. The payment rates tend to be low and there are detailed and, at times, intrusive rules to assess people's family circumstances, income and capital and to compare their income against set rates. Many people who are entitled to means-tested benefits fail to claim them and there are significant error rates by DWP and local authority staff which mean that it is not unusual to find people who have been wrongly refused a means-tested benefit or who are being underpaid.

One major difference between means-tested benefits and the others described in this book is that means-tested benefits are based on what is called 'aggregation'. This means that couples who are living together as husband and wife are jointly assessed; it is their joint needs that are included in working out the amounts and it is their joint income and capital that are counted.

The means-tested benefits are:

- Income Support
- Jobseeker's Allowance (JSA) (Income-Based – there is also a non-means-tested JSA paid for up to six months)
- Pension Credit
- Housing Benefit
- Council Tax Benefit

- Health benefits
- Social Fund
- Tax Credits (social security benefits paid via the income tax system).

Chapter Ten: Income Support (IS) and Income-Based Jobseeker's Allowance (IBJSA)

Income Support (IS) is the most common means-tested benefit. Entitlement is based on meeting one of a number of conditions of entitlement, having less than the maximum amount of capital and having an income, which is less than an 'applicable amount'. The means-test rules for IS and Income-Based Jobseeker's Allowance (IBJSA) are identical. An applicable amount is made up of personal allowances, premiums and some housing costs - not rent but mortgage interest to purchase or improve property, leasehold service charges, etc. People paying rent should claim Housing Benefit.

People who are 60 on low incomes, now claim a new benefit for older people, Pension Credit. Some older people who had incomes which were too high for IS or who had too much capital, now qualify for Pension Credit.

If you have children and you make a new claim for IS after 12 April 2004, you will be treated as follows: If you have not claimed Child Tax Credit (CTC), you will have to also make a claim for this. This will initially be assessed along with the personal allowances and premiums for children. When your CTC is awarded, IS will be re-assessed, removing any elements for children but also ignoring any CTC and Child Benefit which you receive. Effectively IS/IBJSA become benefits for adults.

People already receiving CTC will be assessed with no Income Support elements for children and with CTC and Child Benefit ignored. It is currently planned that as from October 2004, people with children on IS/IBJSA who have children will be helped to claim CTCs and have their IS adjusted accordingly. About 70,000 may be worse off as a result – usually because they have other income or benefits and a small amount of IS.

Pensioners with children (there are 100,000 of them), have to claim CTC on top of their Pension Credit.

Jobseeker's Allowance

People with a disability or long term illness may face difficulty claiming Jobseeker's Allowance unless they are capable of work. It is generally preferable to claim alternative benefits such as Incapacity Benefit and Income Support because often higher levels will be paid and there is less intrusiveness and compulsion.

If you have been refused Incapacity Benefit and you have appealed, you can be accepted as being capable of work for Jobseeker's Allowance while you appeal against a refusal. Alternatively, you can claim IS but this will be paid at a reduced rate while the appeal is still waiting to be heard.

People who have a disability are able to have the labour market conditions for receiving Jobseeker's Allowance relaxed. You can restrict the type of jobs you are willing to look for or accept if the restrictions are reasonable in view of your health or disability. You may need to provide medical evidence for this. If your restrictions are accepted, you don't have to show that you still have a reasonable prospect of obtaining work with these restrictions, a benefit condition that applies to people without a disability or health problem.

If there are difficulties with your restrictions, you should seriously consider claiming Incapacity Benefit instead. If you receive Incapacity Benefit or Income Support, you can still make use of the services of Jobcentre Plus to look for work or training and obtain help and advice from their Disability Employment Advisers. Almost all claims for these benefits now also have to involve a Work Focused Interview (see Chapter 18).

You can find more information about Jobseeker's Allowance in *Inclusion's* Welfare to Work Handbook.

Who is entitled to Income Support/Income-Based Jobseeker's Allowance?

Step One – Basic conditions of entitlement

To qualify for IS, you must:

- be 16 or over (there are no particular restrictions on 16 & 17 year olds receiving Income Support)
- have £8,000 or less in savings or investments. Savings under £3,000 are ignored but you will be treated as having 'tariff income' from savings between £3,000 and £8,000). These capital limits are expected to increase from April 2006
- have £16,000 or less if living permanently in a residential or nursing home (savings under £10,000 are ignored but you will be treated as having 'tariff income' from savings between £10,000 and £16,000)
- not be in full time work (16 hours or more per week) or be the partner of someone in full time work (work of 24 hours or more a week). There are some exceptions to this rule, for example: people with a physical or mental disability whose earnings are reduced because of that disability; childminders, people getting a government training allowance, and people who live in care homes
- not be a full time student in advanced education (there are some exceptions to this, for example, students with a disability and single parents – seek advice)
- pass the 'habitual residence test ', have a right to reside in the UK and not be a Person Subject to Immigration Control.

Step Two – Categories of people

To receive IS, you must be exempt from having to meet the labour market conditions for JSA and if not exempt, you will need to claim JSA and satisfy those conditions.

Examples of people who are exempt from the JSA labour market conditions are:

- lone parents caring for a child under 16
- people who are sick or disabled and unable to work
- carers
- women who are pregnant for 29 weeks and over
- aged 16 – 24 and on a training course as an unwaged trainee.

Step Three – Work out Applicable Amount (the amount for living expenses)

The amount of IS depends on a combination of the following:

- age (people under 25 or 16-17 may have lower rates)
- family size and composition (see paragraph about CTC above)
- ill-health or disability
- other benefits received
- other income
- savings or other capital and
- certain housing costs such as mortgage and loans for repairs and improvements.

The Applicable Amount is: Personal Allowance + Premiums + Housing Costs

If your income is less than the applicable amount, you receive the difference in IS. If your income is more than your Applicable Amount, you are not entitled. But you may still be entitled to other means-tested benefits such as Housing Benefit or Council Tax Benefit.

Personal Allowance

The amount of personal allowance depends on age and whether you are single or a member of a mixed gender couple. If you are aged 16 or 17 you will be assessed using different rates and single people have a lower rate if aged less than 25 (see *Inclusion's* Young Person's Handbook).

Premiums

Premiums are based on your circumstances and those of your partner. Some other benefits (for example Disability Living Allowance) act as a passport to premiums thus increasing the amount of IS payable.

Premiums and conditions of entitlement

Rules about premiums	
Family Premium (non CTC cases). Paid if your family includes a dependant child or young person under 19 who is in full time non-advanced education. (but see note about children and IS). **Disabled Child Premium (non CTC cases).** Your family includes a child for whom DLA is paid or who is registered blind. **Carer's Premium.** You or your partner receives CA or would do if they did not receive an overlapping benefit such as Retirement Pension **Enhanced Disability Premium.** You or a member of the family you claim for receives the higher rate of DLA care component (but see note about children and IS). **Severe Disability Premium.** You are single and receive AA or DLA higher or middle rate care component, have no non-dependants and no one receives CA for you. Or, if a couple, you both receive AA or higher/middle rate DLA care component and with no non-dependants nor carer receiving CA. If one CA is paid, the single SDP is paid to the couple. **Disability Premium.** Paid if you are under 60 and you receive AA or DLA or the long term rate of IB or are registered blind or have been accepted by DWP as incapable of work for at least 52 weeks.	These can all be included in the IS/IBJSA applicable amount on top of any other premiums
Bereavement Premium. If you are single and aged between 55 and 59 on 9/4/01 and received Bereavement Allowance within 8 weeks of claiming IS/IBJSA	This can be awarded on top of a carer premium, severe disability premium or enhanced disability premium but not a disability premium

Housing costs

The rules about housing costs are complex and if you are a homeowner or long leaseholder it is best you to seek advice to ensure that you receive the correct amount. You should also notify your lender. In outline, the housing costs which qualify for the Applicable Amount include:

- mortgage interest for purchasing a home or a share in a home
- interest on certain loans for home improvements and repairs (there are limitations on which repairs and improvements qualify)
- ground rent, feu duty (Scotland) or other charges for long leaseholders
- Crown Tenants' rent
- pitch fee for a tent
- co-ownership payments
- service charges for long leaseholders (for example, minor repairs and maintenance, redecorating or upkeep of grounds).

It is not possible to include:

- capital repayments on a mortgage
- home insurance (except for some long leaseholders if it is included in a service charge)
- mortgage endowment premiums
- water charges

- nor the cost of some loans taken out while on IS/JSA or some loans which were increased while on IS/JSA. However, there are exceptions to some of these – for example, increasing a loan in order to improve accommodation if you are a disabled person, will qualify in certain circumstances.

For IS and IBJSA (not if you or your partner is aged 60 or older), there are waiting periods at the start of a claim when no benefit will be paid towards the interest. The crucial issue is the date that the loan liability arose (i.e. normally the date of exchange of contracts for purchase of the home):

- loan liability arises before 1 October 1995: No interest for first eight weeks of a claim, then 50% of interest for the next 18 weeks, then full standard rate

- loan liability arises on or after 1 October 1995: No interest paid for the first 39 weeks of claim.

You will be treated as having a loan taken out at the earlier date if you are a carer or a lone parent with child(ren) under 16, and your partner has died or you have been left by your partner to cope alone without any support, financial or otherwise, from them.

Because entitlement is based from when a claim is made, it is very important to claim even if you would not otherwise be entitled to IS if the loan interest was not allowed in full in your Applicable Amount.

The amount of loan which qualifies is capped at £100,000 and is also paid direct to a lender every three months.

The amount of housing costs included will be reduced if there are certain non-dependants in the household or if the property is felt to be too large for the claimant.

The subject of mortgages, loans and IS is very complex, so it is important to seek advice to ensure that you are receiving the correct amount of help you are entitled to.

Step Four – Work out income

- almost all benefits count as income against IS. However, Attendance Allowance, Disability Living Allowance, Housing Benefit and Council Tax Benefit are ignored. Working Tax Credit counts in full as income. Certain other income is also ignored, for example:
- Child Tax Credit (CTC)
- the first £10 of a War Pension, Widowed Parent's Allowance, Widowed Mother's Allowance and a War Widow/Widower's Pension
- £10.45 of Child Benefit for a child under a year old and all Child Benefit if CTC has also been claimed
- Guardian's Allowance
- children's earnings (except in the school holiday after leaving school)
- two thirds of earnings as a childminder (an additional earnings disregard is also given on top - see below)
- payments in kind
- payments to third parties on behalf of the claimant and which are not for ordinary living costs – for example a relative paying someone else for a TV licence, mortgage capital or holiday
- volunteer's expenses
- Fostering Allowances (unless a 'reward' element is paid)
- Education Maintenance Allowances
- voluntary payments for things which are not classed as ordinary living expenses.

Some income is partly ignored. For example:

- £10 of maintenance received
- £10 of a student loan
- £20 of a regular charitable or voluntary payment for ordinary living expenses

Earnings

Net earnings from employment or self-employment (i.e. after any tax, National Insurance and half of any pension contributions) are counted as income after the following disregards. The most common are:

- £20 if someone qualifies for the disability premium, severe disability premium, or carer's premium (disregard is on carer's earnings only) or is a lone parent
- £20 for certain occupations – for example, retained firefighter, lifeboat staff, territorial or reserve forces
- £10 for a couple
- £20 per lodger plus half of anything above this for providing board and lodging
- £5 for anyone else.

Most other forms of income are counted in full, including occupational pensions.

Weekly 'tariff income' is assumed from any savings between:

- £3,000 and £8,000 if aged under 60; £1 for every £250 or part of £250 above £3,000
- £10,000 and £16,000 if in residential or nursing care; £1 for every £250 or part of £250 above £10,000.

This is considerably higher than the true amounts paid in interest on savings. However, see the more generous treatment of income from capital for Tax Credit and Pension Credit.

Income Support Calculation for a single person: case study

Helen is single, aged 40 and has been on Incapacity Benefit for 18 months. She has no capital and is a tenant.

In this example, Helen has £2.60 too much income to qualify for Income Support because the long term rate of Incapacity Benefit is higher than the total of the single person's personal allowance and the disability premium. However, if she successfully claimed CA or DLA middle/higher rate care component, or if she had qualifying housing costs, she would then be able to qualify for Income Support.

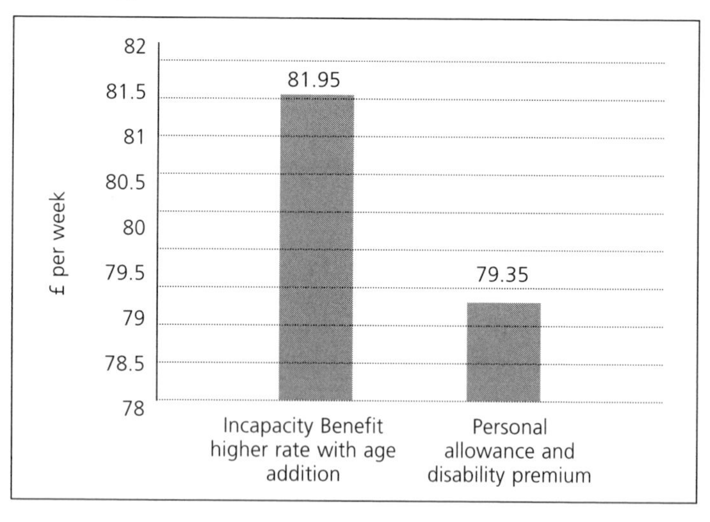

Claiming

IS should be claimed as soon as entitlement arises because backdating is very difficult.

IS can be backdated for up to one month if you could not reasonably have been expected to claim sooner and there have been particular circumstances for example, postage delays, transport difficulties, death of a close relative or recent separation from a partner. Backdating is also possible for up to three months if one of the following specified reasons applies:

- you have a learning, language or literacy difficulty (but if you have an appointee, see page 13, the appointee has to show that you fall into this or another category)
- you are deaf or blind
- you are a carer, or dealing with a domestic emergency and it was not reasonably practical for you to get help to make your claim from anyone else
- because of information given by the DWP, you thought you were not entitled to benefit
- because of written information given by a Citizens Advice Bureau, advice worker or other professional adviser, solicitor, doctor or local authority, you thought you were not entitled to benefit
- a decision maker was given written information about your income or capital from your employer or bank, and as a result thought that you were not entitled to benefit
- you could not get to a DWP office because of bad weather.

How to claim

A claim can be triggered by phoning or writing to the local Jobcentre Plus office and asking to claim IS. You are then sent a claim pack (A1) which you should complete and return as soon as possible.

When you are sent the IS claim pack, it is date stamped with the date of initial contact and you then have 28 days (or longer if you have a good reason), to complete and return it together with supporting evidence which is reasonably required to assess the claim, (for example, payslips, evidence of savings). The form should be completed and returned, even if evidence is not immediately to hand with a note explaining why any evidence is not available. It is important to complete and return the form as soon as possible to avoid undue delay in receiving IS. If there are difficulties obtaining evidence or if the person has gone over the 28 day limit, seek independent advice about what to do.

Important points

- the IS claim pack includes a claim form for Housing and Council Tax Benefits (HCTB1). However, if you are renting from a private landlord, you may be asked to provide additional information

- it can sometimes be difficult to estimate if you are entitled to IS – for example, if the amount of capital or income you have is unclear or if you have a mortgage or housing loan. If in doubt, make a claim anyway

- if you are counted as having tariff income from capital, you should inform the DWP each time your capital decreases or increases, even by small amounts as you might have gone up or down from the 'band' that you are in for tariff income. For example, a person with £6,260 in savings need only spend £10 to drop into a lower band of tariff income, worth an extra £1 per week to them

- certain things don't count as capital. For example, the value of a home which the person lives in, money from the sale of a home which is intended to be used to buy another within six months or longer where reasonable, arrears of IS, AA/DLA, Tax Credits, JSA, Housing and Council Tax Benefits for up to a year after they have been received, arrears of means tested benefits over £5000 paid because of official error ignored for over a year, the value of personal possessions and personal injury trust funds. It is expected that Child Trust Funds will be ignored

- capital includes shares, savings, premium bonds and other investments that you and any partner have. Children's capital is ignored but if the child has capital of £3000 or more, there will be no entitlement to premiums and allowances for that child

- you can be counted as still having capital which you have deliberately disposed of in order to receive or increase means-tested benefits. Seek independent advice if caught by this rule

- people who carry out an unpaid service for another (except bona fide volunteers) may be caught by the 'notional income' rule and treated as having an income they don't actually have. Seek independent advice

- unmarried, opposite gender couples (including people who have a relationship with someone who stays from time to time) may have difficulty with the Living Together as husband and wife rules

- however, couples who have separated but who are still under the same roof, may still qualify as separate households and be able to receive IS in their own right

- people with a mortgage who claim IS/JSA should inform their lender as soon as possible. There is a Code of Practice to prevent evictions in such cases. However, the various restrictions on help with loans and mortgages can still mean that mortgage arrears mount up. If you have a loan or mortgage, it is always worth seeking advice to check that the amount allowed in their IS/JSA has been correctly calculated

- people with arrears of housing costs, fuel, water charges, Council Tax, fines, compensation orders and maintenance can have deductions made from their IS/JSA to pay current liabilities and a small prescribed amount towards the debt (Third Party Deduction). This is an extremely important safeguard to prevent imprisonment, loss of home or loss of utilities, but the DWP may need persuasion to assist. Seek independent advice if necessary

- it is not uncommon for the Carer, Disabled Child and Severe Disability Premiums to be missed by the DWP when they assess someone's IS/JSA. This is especially true if you are already on IS when you receive the qualifying benefit such as Attendance Allowance which attracts the extra premium. As the DWP have procedures in place which mean other relevant parts of the benefits system are routinely told when these qualifying benefits are awarded, the person should be able to get all arrears due to them, but it might need a challenge for the DWP to pay up!

- the rules about IS and income based JSA are complex and people can often hit problems. There is also a high error rate by DWP staff, so it is often worth checking that the correct amount is being paid. When underpayments have occurred because of official error, arrears should be paid and in some cases a compensation payment is also possible (but this should be specifically requested as it will not be made unless asked for). When overpayments occur, the DWP often simply ask for the overpaid money back. However, if the overpayment was caused by official error, the DWP need to prove that the claimant has either 'misrepresented' or failed to disclose a material fact

- if you receive IS/IBJSA, you are also entitled to free prescriptions and other health benefits and free school meals. In many areas, local authorities also give free or reduced access to sports and leisure facilities

- special rules apply to people in residential and nursing homes

- people aged 16 and 17 have the same entitlement to IS as

anyone else if they are exempt from the JSA labour market conditions. This includes, for example, young people (including those looked after by a local authority) who qualify because they have a disability, or are a lone parent. One group of 16 and 17 year olds who qualify are those in full time non-advanced education who are estranged from their parents and have no one acting in their place. Jobcentre Plus staff may try to contact parents to verify this. Note that there are two IS rates for those under 18 - the higher rate is paid to those who live away from home or who are disabled

- people receiving help with mortgage or loan interest in their IS, may not know that if they go off IS for more than 12 weeks, they will have to serve the waiting period again before they receive this help. However, for many people taking up jobs, they can be off IS for up to 52 weeks without having to repeat their waiting period

- the government estimates that £4.45 billion in means-tested benefits is unclaimed each year which shows that many people on low incomes who should claim them, don't

- people making a new IS claim in Jobcentre Plus areas and all new lone parents, will have to attend a Work Focused Interview with Jobcentre Plus staff (but this can be deferred or waived for good reason). They do not have to take up any work or training options discussed but will normally have to attend the interview

- an IS claim by a lone parent will trigger a Child Support Agency maintenance application. Seek advice if this could cause difficulty (preferably before the Agency become involved) as it may be possible to stop a maintenance application going ahead if it would put a parent or a child at risk and in some cases a CTC claim may be preferable.

Chapter Eleven: Pension Credit (PC)

What is it?

Pension Credit (PC) has nothing to do with Tax Credits. It is a new benefit for people aged 60 or over which was introduced on 6th October 2003. It replaced Income Support for pensioners (also known as Minimum Income Guarantee or MIG). PC is means-tested and has two elements - a Guarantee Credit for people aged 60 or over and a Savings Credit for people aged 65 or over. People aged 65 or over will be able to get both elements, depending upon their income.

People will be able to claim up until 6 October 2004 and have benefit backdated to 6 October 2003. Claims after that date can be backdated for up to 12 months.

The major differences between PC and MIG are that there are no savings limits, tariff income is less compared to Income Support and occupational or private pensions and savings may increase the amount of PC in payment. There is also no 16 hour work limit as there is for Income Support.

Who is entitled?

Step One - Basic conditions of entitlement

To qualify for PC, you must:

- be aged 60 or over (65 for Savings Credit) and
- pass the habitual residence in United Kingdom test and other immigration conditions.

Step Two – Work out Appropriate Amount and income

The amount of Pension Credit depends on a combination of the following:

- age
- family size and composition
- ill-health, disability or caring responsibilities
- other benefits received
- other income
- tariff income from savings or other capital
- certain housing costs (e.g. mortgages and loans for repair and improvement– same rules as Income Support).

The rules about income are the same as those for Income Support, except for the rules about tariff income from capital.

The PC means-test formula is in two stages:

For the Guarantee Credit, the appropriate amount is made up of a standard amount (£105.45 for a single person; £160.95 for a couple), plus extra amounts if the person is severely disabled or a carer, plus certain housing costs, such as mortgage interest (all these are calculated using the same rules as Income Support, except that the standard amounts replace the personal allowances). This is known as the appropriate minimum guarantee. From this figure, the DWP deduct income, in much the same way as Income Support is calculated. This means that benefits like Attendance and Disability Living Allowances are ignored (as is any Child Benefit or Child Tax Credit), while Retirement Pension and occupational pensions, etc count in full.

No additional amounts for children are included in the PENSION CREDIT calculation (CTC must be claimed instead).

If you have savings over £6,000 (£10,000 if in a care home), the DWP assume £1 per week tariff income for every £500 or part of £500 above the threshold. There is no upper savings limit.

If you have an income which is less than the appropriate amount, you receive the difference as the guarantee element of PC. This is very similar to an Income Support calculation.

Case Study

George is single, 67 and lives alone. His appropriate amount is £105.45 per week as he is not disabled nor a carer. His income is Retirement Pension of £79.60 per week and £12 occupational pension. He has savings of £8,200. This gives a tariff income of £5 per week. His total income for PC purposes is therefore £96.60 per week. He will have entitlement to the Guarantee Credit element of PC worth £8.85 per week.

If George was severely disabled (e.g. getting Attendance Allowance and living alone with no-one receiving Carer's Allowance for looking after him), the appropriate amount would be £44.15 per week higher, resulting in a similar increase in the PC payment.

Because George is aged over 65 and has savings and an occupational pension, he will also get the Savings Credit element in addition to the Guarantee Credit.

Step Three – Work out Savings Credit

This is more difficult to calculate than the Guarantee Credit element and is not just based on savings. It only applies to those aged 65 or older. The Savings Credit threshold is £79.60 for single people and £127.25 for a couple (i.e. the same amount as the full Retirement Pension). Work out how much qualifying income you have between this threshold and the basic Guarantee Credit amount (£105.45/£160.95). You then calculate 60% of that figure. This is the amount of Savings

Credit you will receive, up to a maximum of £15.51 for a single person and £20.22 for a couple.

However, if your income is above the Guarantee Credit level, the Savings Credit is reduced by 40% of the amount above the Guarantee Credit. As you can see, this is a very complicated process because Savings Credit rises and then falls as income rises above the threshold.

Case Study

George, from the example above, has Retirement Pension of £79.60 and £17 of other income. This puts him £17.00 above the Savings Credit threshold (known as excess income). 60% of that excess is £10.20 and so he gets £10.20 Savings Credit on top of the £8.85 he gets from the guarantee element of Pension Credit.

If he had an occupational pension of £25 a week, he would not be entitled to the Guarantee Credit, but would receive £2.49 a week Savings Credit (i.e. 60% of the amount of income above the appropriate minimum guarantee).

How to claim

You can get a claim form by phoning 0800 99 1234. The claim form can be completed over the phone on this number, but you can also ask to complete it yourself, or else ask for a visit by the Pension Service in order to do so. Claim forms are also available from the DWP website, DWP Pension Service outlets and advice agencies, but people who have sent in claim forms without phoning first have experienced problems with their claim not be dealt with, so it is best to phone first.

If you claim before October 2004, it will be automatically backdated to 6 October 2003. Claims made after this date will be backdated for up to twelve months and then from October 2005, it is intended that they are backdated for up to three months.

Important points

- Pension Credit is officially called State Pension Credit
- it will often be difficult to estimate who is entitled to PC – for example, if the amount of capital or income you have is unclear. If in doubt, make a claim anyway
- if you are counted as having tariff income from capital, you need to notify the DWP each time your capital decreases or increases, even by small amounts as you might have gone up or down from the 'band' that you are in for tariff income. For example, a person with £6,509 in savings need only spend £10 to drop into a lower band of tariff income, worth an extra £1 per week to them
- most Pension Credit work is being done at new regional Pension Service offices, some of which are mostly staffed by people new to benefits work. There have been many reports of staff having difficulty with the more complex areas of entitlement
- claims made via the Pensions Service will mainly be done over the telephone, with the Pensions Service sending the form to the claimant for signature
- pensioners who have been turned down for IS/MIG in the past will need encouraging to try again for PC. Some will still be refused. Because Pension credit is increased in line with earnings while almost all other benefits are increased in line only with prices, an extra 100,000 older people will become entitled to Pension Credit each year
- people aged 60 or over who received Income Support immediately before 6 October 2003, did not have to make a claim for PC – they were automatically transferred onto the new benefit

- if your income is less than the Savings Credit threshold you are not entitled to Savings Credit, even if your income is very low. This will particularly affect those with gaps in the national insurance record and is more likely to affect women than men – so there may be grounds for a legal challenge on sex discrimination grounds

- several million national insurance records are unmatched by the Inland Revenue's computer system. People may be informed incorrectly that their Retirement Pension is lower than it ought to be

- if you get the guarantee element of PC, you will get full HB/CTB (even if savings are over £16,000 HB threshold or if they have Savings Credit in addition)

- if you receive only the savings element of PC will have this taken into account as income for HB/CTB purposes

- PC for those aged 65 or over, can be awarded for up to 5 years at a time, although you can ask for a reassessment if your circumstances change e.g. you become disabled and qualify for the severe disability elements or your other income or capital decreases

- if your retirement provision or capital increases you do not have to notify the DWP and won't reduce their PC. This is designed to simplify administration. Retirement provision includes retirement pensions, annuities and capital. Other changes in income should be reported

- PC is quite separate from Tax Credits. People aged 60 or over who have children will also have to claim Child Tax Credit as well as Pension Credit

- the take-up rate of Pension Credit is running at about 60% at the time of writing and the government target is to get just 73% of those who are entitled to receive it.

Chapter Twelve: Working Tax Credit (WTC) and Child Tax Credit (CTC)

April 2003 saw the introduction of:

- Working Tax Credit and
- Child Tax Credit

Administered by the Inland Revenue, tax credits separate means-tested support for adults and children. Instead of claiming one benefit for the entire family, all income-based support for children will be streamlined into one payment – the Child Tax Credit. This will be paid direct to the person mainly responsible for caring for the children. It is planned that from October 2004, people with children receiving Income Support or income based Jobseeker's Allowance will gradually be moved onto Child Tax Credits to replace the child related elements of Income Support/income based Jobseeker's Allowance. These two benefits will then be recalculated ignoring the Child Tax Credit and Child Benefit and most people will either be better off or no worse off, but some will lose out. The process of moving people will be done on a phased basis.

Adults will still be able to claim Income Support or Income-Based Jobseeker's Allowance for themselves (and Income Support for housing costs). Alternatively, adults may be entitled to Working Tax Credit, for low income working households, with or without children.

Tax Credit awards are based on annual income from the previous tax year. There is no capital limit and only actual, taxable income of more than £300 a year from capital is counted (with income from tax free sources such as Individual Savings Accounts ignored).

Working Tax Credit

Who is entitled?

Working Tax Credit is for:

- people with dependent children and working at least 16 hours a week
- people with a disability working at least 16 hours a week
- people aged 25 or over and working at least 30 hours a week
- people aged 50 or over working at least 16 hours a week.

You must also meet the following general conditions:

- at the date of claim, you are working, or due to start work within seven days and the work is expected to last for at least four weeks
- if you have a disability, you must also have a defined disadvantage in finding and keeping work and also receive or have recently received a benefit for a disability or ill-health
- the work is done for payment (or the expectation of payment) and
- you are not subject to immigration control and you are ordinarily resident in the UK.

Working Tax Credit is made up of a basic element, and additional elements for:

- couples and lone parents
- people working 30 hours or more a week

- disabled workers
- people aged 50 or over returning to work after a 6 month period on benefit and
- the childcare element to help with childcare costs and which is paid direct to the main carer.

Working Tax Credit is paid to employees through their pay packet and directly to the self employed via a bank account. However, the government is consulting about ending the need for employers to pay WTC.

Where a lone parent or both partners in a couple work at least 16 hours a week, or where one partner works and the other is disabled or long term sick, families will be eligible for the childcare element. It is worth up to 70% of eligible child care costs to a limit of £135 for one child (equal to a weekly credit of up to £94.50) and £200 for two or more children (equal to a weekly credit of up to £140). To calculate these, childcare costs are averaged out. Claimants need to keep the Inland Revenue informed of changes in childcare arrangements and costs (£10 or more a week for four or more weeks) as this can affect the amount of Credit payable.

Childcare costs which are eligible for the child care element include payments to:

- registered childminders, nurseries, play schemes or out of school clubs
- certain schools or other establishments exempt from registration
- providers of childcare for children aged 8 and over, which are approved by specifically accredited organisations
- Approved childcare provided in own home.

Note: first time parents who were working at least 16 hours a week before going on maternity, paternity or adoption leave can claim WTC from the date of birth or adoption of their first child and mothers on paid maternity leave can receive help with the costs of childcare for their new babies.

	April 1999	October 1999	April 2004
Family 1 child, full-time work (35 hours)	£182	£200	£248
Family 1 child, part-time work (16 hours)	£136	£144	£190
Single person, no children, 25 or over, full-time work (35 hours)	£113	£113	£160
Couple, no children, 25 or over, full-time work (35 hours)	£117	£117	£190
Disabled person (single), working full-time (35 hours)	£139	£155	£201
Disabled person (single), working part-time (16 hours)	£109	£112	£142

(Source: HM Treasury Pre Budget Report Dec 2003)

Child Tax Credit

Who is entitled?

Child Tax Credit (CTC) can be claimed by anyone aged 16 or over, responsible for a child who normally lives with them and who is:

- aged under 16 years of age
- aged 16 (if they leave school at 16, CTC is paid until the beginning of September following their 16th birthday – but see below)
- aged less than 19 years of age and in full-time, non-advanced education.

It will be paid direct to the main carer for the children in the family. In the case of shared care arrangements, it is paid to the person with main responsibility for the child. In some circumstances a young person aged under 18 who has ceased full-time education within 20 weeks can be treated as a qualifying child if they have registered for work or training with the Connexions/careers service. If a young person enters paid work for 24 or more hours a week or they receive Income Support or Jobseeker's Allowance in their own right, they can no longer be included in a CTC or WTC claim.

A separate child element will be payable for each child in the household. There is a disability element for children with a disability.

CTC is made up of:

- a basic family element, and
- a higher family element (baby element) for a child(ren) under one
- a child element, for each child
- a disabled child element, for each child who gets Disability Living Allowance
- an enhanced disabled child element, for each child who gets Disability Living Allowance at the higher rate care component.

To calculate Tax Credits, work out how many days in the relevant period (i.e. the length of time the award will run for), add up all the elements which apply to find the maximum possible Tax Credit. Then add up the income.

Tax Credit entitlement is assessed on an annual basis but is calculated using the length of the relevant period. People who do not receive Income Support or income-based Jobseeker's

Allowance are entitled to maximum Tax Credits if their gross income is below a set threshold of £5,060 for people who are entitled to WTC or £13,480 for if they are entitled to CTC only (maximum Tax Credits being payable to those receiving IS/IBJSA).

If income exceeds the threshold, Tax Credit entitlement tapers away by 37p for every £1 by which income above the threshold. The family element of CTC is retained until income exceeds the second threshold of £50,000, at which point it begins to taper away at the rate of £1 in every £15 (i.e. 6.67%).

Once an award has been made it can run until the end of the tax year. However, if there is a change affecting the amount of Tax Credit due, the award can be adjusted from the date of the change.

The higher threshold for Child Tax Credit means that everyone over 16 with dependent children (so long as they are not subject to immigration control and are ordinarily resident in the UK) gets at least some family element of Child Tax Credit if their annual household income is less than £58,175 (£62,000 if they have a child under one).

The definition of income for Tax Credits is based on the income tax system. As a general rule, income is taken into account if it is taxable and ignored if it is not. Gross, rather than net income, is taken into account. The following don't count as income:

- Child Benefit
- Disability Living and Attendance Allowances
- maintenance (whether by a Court order or not, including maintenance for child and/or spouse)
- Housing Benefit, Council Tax Benefit, Income Support, Income-Based Jobseeker's Allowance and Pension Credit
- Maternity Allowance and up to £102 per week of Statutory Maternity Pay.

For the first year only, claims made from April 2003, were provisionally assessed on income from the tax year two years before - i.e. 2001/2. After this, relevant income will be used to assess all future claims. Relevant income is:

- current year's income, if this is less than previous year's income
- current year's income, minus £2,500, if the current year's income exceeds previous years by more than £2,500
- in any other case, previous year's income.

With two main exceptions, there is no obligation to inform the Inland Revenue of any changes of income during the year, only at the year end. If income falls, claimants can ask the Inland Revenue to reassess the award during the year, or wait until the end of the year when the award is reconciled. Any Tax Credit due would then be paid in a lump sum. If income rises by less than £2,500 in the current year, there is no change to the WTC/CTC award.

If income rises by more than £2,500 in the current year, the WTC/CTC award is reduced. Although the first £2,500 of an income rise is ignored in the current year for that year's award, it is not ignored when the award is renewed in the following tax year.

How to claim

Claims for the new Tax Credits can either be made online at www.inlandrevenue.gov.uk/taxcredits or by post. Help with filling in the claim form is available from a dedicated telephone helpline (0845 6095000) and on the website. There is a single claim form for both types of Tax Credit and awards will run for a maximum of 12 months i.e. up to end of the tax year.

At the end of the tax year you are sent a renewal form asking you to confirm your true income. This reconciles (corrects) the award for the year just ending and forms the basis for the next award.

The date of claim is the date that a claim form is received at an Inland Revenue office, or received on-line by the Inland Revenue computer. Claims will be automatically backdated for up to three months from the date of claim where you, the claimant, have met all the conditions of entitlement during that period.

CTC is paid directly by the Inland Revenue to the main carer of the children and people can choose whether to receive Tax Credits weekly or four weekly. It is paid directly into their bank account.

Important points

- WTC and CTC count as income for Housing and Council Tax Benefits. This means that many will either have little or no HB/CTB entitlement and will have to pay these bills. It is the amount of Tax Credit actually paid, rather than what the claimant is entitled to, which is taken into account. This means that HB/CTB will not need to take account of retrospective over and under payments of WTC/CTC and they should not delay processing a HB/CTB claim while a Tax Credit claim is being assessed

- you should notify your local authority if you receive Tax Credits, because there is currently no automatic process for this to occur and you may otherwise be overpaid Housing Benefit/Council Tax Benefit

- if work ends, so does WTC (unless for maternity)

- some parents who only receive a very small amount of Income Support (to top-up child support for example) may be better-off switching to CTC before September 2004. This has to be worked out very carefully, looking at Tax Credit entitlement as well as possible loss of maximum Housing Benefit, free school meals, etc. If you think you are in this situation, seek advice.

- people receiving Pension Credit, Income Support or Income-Based Job Seeker's Allowance are passported through to maximum Child Tax Credit

- if childcare costs reduce by more than £10 a week for four or more weeks in a row, the Inland Revenue must be notified. Failure to do that could mean a penalty of up to £300

- most other changes (including increases in income of more than £2,500 a year), can be left until the end of year reconciliation but it may be better to ask for recalculations as they occur in order to avoid large overpayments or to ensure that you have an adequate income at the time you need it most

- administration of Tax Credit is proving to be very difficult. Apart from delays in payment, some of the Tax Credit award notices are misleading. This can be very important when various elements of Tax Credits are used as a passport to benefits or services. It is therefore important to check the notices carefully and seek independent advice if necessary

- it is possible to receive immediate payments from the Inland Revenue where there is delay in making payment

- payment is made direct into bank accounts unless there are exceptional circumstances

- the method of assessing tax credits on annual income is very prone to creating overpayments. In addition, there have been many instances of official error causing overpayments. The Inland Revenue has a broad discretion to waive recovery of overpayments but they have set out their policy in a Code of Practice (CoP 26), which, has examples of when hardship occurs, or if the claimant could not reasonably be expected to realise that they were being overpaid as an acceptable reason for not recovering an overpayment. In law the broader discretion is more important than the Code of

Practice. However, while there is no formal right of appeal about recovery of an overpayment, it maybe worth appealing using human rights arguments about the right to a fair hearing to challenge this and overpayments can also be challenged by taking up action via an MP and/or by judicial review and also by complaint to the Inland Revenue Adjudication

- it is essential to use computer based packages for calculating Tax Credits and also for calculating the effect of Credits on Housing Benefit/Council Tax Benefit. Examples are the Lisson Grove Benefits Program at www.lgbp.co.uk and the Ferret Maximiser program at www.ferret.co.uk.

Chapter Thirteen: Housing Benefit (HB) and Council Tax Benefit (CTB)

These are means-tested benefits to help with the costs of rent and/or Council Tax. In Northern Ireland, it is possible to claim a domestic rate rebate which is worked out in a similar way to Council Tax Benefit (CTB) but which is paid as part of HB. These benefits may be received both by people who are in work or out of work, though people on Income Support or Income-Based Jobseeker's Allowance (or equivalent income levels) receive maximum help.

HB and CTB are often reduced if someone lives with the claimant, such as an adult son or daughter. Housing Benefit (HB) can also be reduced if the rent is considered to be too high.

The Government has been trying out a new form of HB in ten pilot areas based on Standard Local Housing Allowances for private tenants in the deregulated sector. These are fixed amounts, based on the size of the person's household, irrespective of the rent charged. If the allowance is higher than the rent, the tenant makes a profit, but if it's lower, they have to find the balance themselves. The government currently intends to roll this scheme out nationally from April 2005 and to extend the range of tenants who are covered. They are also planning to align the income rules more closely with those for Tax Credits.

Standards of administration of HB and CTB around the country vary tremendously.

Who is entitled?

You must:

- be liable to make payments for occupying your home (this includes licence fees, board and lodging charges and similar payments, not just rent) and/or Council Tax. Verbal contracts to make rent payments also count

- have less than £16,000 savings. For every £250, or part of £250 above £3,000 (if under 60) or £6,000 (if over 60), you are treated as having a weekly income of £1. However, for those aged 60 or over the rules changed on 6 October 2003 so that only every £500 over £6000 will have £1 tariff income. People who receive the Pension Credit because of the guarantee credit can have more than £16,000 capital and still qualify for HB

- not pay rent to a close relative whom you live with

- not live in a registered care home

- not be disqualified because you are not habitually resident in the UK nor subject to immigration conditions on your stay

- not be a full-time student in higher education (there are exceptions, for example, those with children or a disability, non-student partners).

How to work out entitlement

Step One – Work out Applicable Amount.

This is the same as working out the Applicable Amount for Income Support, except that:

- there are different personal allowances for single people aged 16 – 24 and lone parents under 18

- an additional premium paid during a baby's first year

- different personal allowances for people aged 60 or over from 6 October 2003 (to mirror the introduction of Pension Credit) and with partial disregard of savings credit

- people awarded Income Support, Income-Based Jobseeker's Allowance or the guarantee credit of Pension Credit (even if you have too much capital for HB/CTB) are passported onto maximum HB/CTB.

Step Two – Work out income.

- the rules about income and capital are almost identical to Income Support except, for example:
- the higher capital limits mentioned above
- £25 disregard on lone parent's earnings (if not on Income Support)
- a further £11.90 disregard for people working 16 or more hours a week (previously this was 30 hours per week)
- inclusion of 70% of childcare costs up to £135 for one child under 15 or £200 for more than one child as an additional earnings disregard for some people working at least 16 hours a week
- £15 of Widowed Parent's or Mother's Allowance
- £15 of any maintenance paid for children
- from 6 October 2003 for people aged 60 plus, earnings are ignored.

Step Three – Work out eligible rent and Council Tax (General Rates in Northern Ireland)

The rent that is eligible for HB purposes is not necessarily the rent that your landlord charges. For example, it must not include any charges for water, fuel, meals or services such as support and counselling. If fuel or meals are included in the rent, the eligible rent is reduced by fixed amounts (or by the amount estimated by the landlord for fuel consumption).

The cost of counselling and support included in rent is now met by the local Supporting People Fund paying the landlord direct.

The eligible rent can also be reduced if the property is rented from a private landlord and the rent is above levels set by a Rent Officer's assessment (in Northern Ireland the Housing Executive decides this) or it is unreasonably large. For most childless single people under the age of 25, the eligible rent for private tenants is restricted to the equivalent rent to a room in a shared house. There are exceptions to this rule for example, if aged under 22 and previously looked after by a local authority or severely disabled. If your eligible rent has been restricted it is essential to seek independent advice and help with appealing. Also see the note below about Discretionary Housing Payments.

If you are thinking of renting privately, you can obtain a pre-tenancy determination from the HB office which will show the maximum level to be met for HB.

For CTB, the maximum eligible is the amount of Council Tax which the you or any partner are liable for. If you are not liable for Council Tax (for example, you live in someone else's home, provided that you are not their partner), the person who is liable may be able to receive a Second Adult Rebate, even if they otherwise have too much income or capital.

Step Four – Work out the HB and CTB

If your income is at or below your Applicable Amount (or you get IS, income based SSA or the guarantee credit of PC), then you receive 100% of your eligible rent and/or Council Tax. This is credited to the rent account for Council tenants. CTB is also paid straight into your Council Tax account. In some cases, private tenants' HB can be paid direct to their landlord (but in arrear, which causes difficulties).

If your income is above your applicable amount:

- work out the amount above your Applicable Amount (the excess income)
- work out 65% and 20% of the excess income

- take the resulting 65% and 20% figures off the eligible rent and Council Tax figures respectively to find how much benefit will be paid. A minus figure indicates that no benefit is payable

Case Study

A single person paying £60 per week eligible rent and £15 per week Council Tax with income of £125 per week and an Applicable Amount of £105.45:

Excess income is £19.55 (£125 minus £105.45)

65% of excess is £12.71

20% of excess is £3.91

HB is £60 minus £12.71 = £47.29

CTB is £15 minus £3.91 = £11.09

Step Five – Finally, reduce benefit by any Non-Dependant's Deduction

If you have other people normally residing in your home, your HB and/or CTB are often reduced by Non-Dependant Deductions as it is assumed that they will contribute towards the rent and/or Council Tax.

A non-dependant is someone who normally resides with the person who is claiming benefit and does so on a non-commercial basis and for example, who is also not your partner nor a dependant child or young person nor someone who just shares communal areas.

Some other non-dependants in the home are also not included, so no deduction should be made from the HB or CTB for people who are:

- on a young person's training scheme

- full-time students
- on Income Support (but only if under 25 for HB).

Having certain non-dependants in the home mean that no deduction should be made from the HB or CTB. These include people who are:

- under 18
- on a young person's training scheme
- full-time students
- on Income Support (but only if under 25 for HB)
- in hospital for more than 12 months.

The amount of deduction depends on the non-dependants' income and their age.

Non-dependant deductions should not be made when the person claiming HB/CTB or their partner is registered as blind or receives Attendance Allowance or Disability Living Allowance care component.

If you receive Pension Credit, no non-dependant deduction will be made until the non-dependant has been normally residing for at least 26 weeks.

Discretionary Housing Payments

Each local authority has a fixed budget to allow them to pay Discretionary Housing Payments up to 100% of HB or CTB, usually for a time limited period if the local authority are satisfied that there is a need for additional help with housing costs (and each year, most local authorities underspend their Discretionary Housing Payment budgets). These are particularly useful where non-dependant deductions are causing difficulty or in other cases where less than full payment of HB or CTB causes difficulties. For example, this could include situations where the eligible rent has been restricted, there has been a reduction in benefit or there is debt, illness or family stress.

Discretionary Housing Payments have to be applied for and normally this can be done by letter, preferably setting out the case and with supporting evidence though the local authority may have an additional form for completion. You cannot appeal to a Tribunal if a Discretionary Housing Payment is refused, but there are rights to have a negative decision reviewed and it may be possible to challenge a refusal through Judicial Review proceedings in the Courts.

How to claim

Claims for HB should be made as soon as entitlement arises because the claim is not effective until it has been received by the HB service. Claims can be backdated for up to 52 weeks if you can show you have good cause for claiming late.

If you receive Income Support or income based Jobseeker's Allowance you should complete the HCTB1 form enclosed with the claim form. It is important to enclose as much evidence as possible with the claim form in order to speed up decision making on the claim.

If you are not on Income Support nor income based Jobseeker's Allowance, the claim is made direct to the Council responsible for paying HB and CTB on a HB/CTB claim form (Councils usually have their own forms for this).

If you are aged 60 or older you can use a shorter claim form HCTB1(PC) when you claim Pension Credit. The form is returned direct to the local authority, but the Local Authority won't know the amount of Pension Credit awarded and mistakes may arise as a result.

From April 2004, HB is no longer awarded for a fixed period but will be an open-ended award which may be ended if someone goes off IS/IBJSA. Other changes will be treated as a change in circumstances. This will improve benefits processing times but may increase problems with overpayments.

Important issues

- delays in processing HB claims are common but there is a clear legal requirement for local authorities to make interim payments to private tenants after 14 days

- it can be classed as an abuse of process (a legal term) for a local authority to both delay HB and to also take action for rent arrears caused by their delay. Seek legal advice

- an award of HB or CTB stops if someone's Income Support or Income-Based JSA stops. The local authority should invite them to make a new claim for HB, however, this does not always happen

- HB and CTB can be suspended when there is doubt about entitlement or if information to support a claim is not forthcoming

- administration of HB can be disrupted when non-dependants' circumstances change as it may mean that a different rate of non-dependants' deduction should apply

- if you are under 18 years of age, you can still receive HB, provided that you are liable to pay rent

- if non-dependants refuse to provide proof of their income details, it can disrupt the main claimant's HB/CTB. In law, this is wrong, as it is only a delay or failure by the person claiming to provide evidence which gives grounds for this

- there can be problems when someone is absent from their home, has to pay rent on two properties at once, has an empty property or delays moving into a new property. Seek advice

- 70% of tenants in the de-regulated private sector have HB restricted

- keep copies of correspondence on HB/CTB and obtain written receipts for all evidence that is provided. It is not unknown, especially in the less well-organised local authorities, for communications to be mislaid or for them to state that they have not been received. This is a particular issue because the Verification Framework for HB means that local authorities ask to see original copies of evidence, including evidence of identity and National Insurance numbers. Local authorities can be flexible with some people without original evidence - for example those fleeing domestic violence or who are homeless

- water charges in Scotland are automatically reduced for people who receive CTB if their charges are more than £240 a year (2004/05). In England and Wales, people on a metered water supply who have 3 or more children or certain long term illnesses, can have the charge capped if they also receive a means tested benefit or Working Tax Credit or Council Tax Credit of more than the family element.

Chapter Fourteen: Disability reductions for Council Tax

You can have your home put into a lower Council Tax valuation band if your disability means that you meet certain rules and this can be backdated. You don't have to own your home to qualify and there is a similar scheme in Northern Ireland where the General Rates system still operates.

You can qualify for a Council Tax Disability Reduction if you or someone who lives with you is substantially and permanently disabled and you have:

- an additional bathroom, kitchen for the disabled person
- additional space for a wheelchair
- a room (not a bathroom, kitchen or toilet) mostly used by the disabled person.

In a recent case (Sandwell Metropolitan Borough Council, R (on the application of) v Perks & Anor [2003] EWHC 1749 (Admin) 08 July 2003), it was held that there should be a close link between the disability and the need to use a room. This means that you may qualify for a reduction if the disabled person has to use another bedroom because of their disability, an extra bedroom is needed by a carer or where a room has to be used as a bedroom by the disabled person and it prevents others in the home using it.

You can appeal to a Valuation Tribunal if your claim for a Council Tax Disability Reduction is refused.

Council Tax is partly based on an amount for two adults residing in the property. If only one adult lives in the property, you qualify for a discount and also if there are two adults living in your home, you may get a discount by having the other person ignored for Council Tax purposes if they fall into one of several categories including:

- an adult is who is severely mentally impaired
- certain carers (but not partners nor parents of disabled children under 18)
- students or trainees.

A reduction in Council Tax may not produce immediate gains for someone in England and Wales who is receiving maximum CTB and who is likely to remain so, but in Scotland it may reduce their water charges. A reduction will also help if someone leaves means tested benefits – for example, they go into full-time work.

New legislation (s. 76 Local Government Act 2003) governs local authorities in England and Wales allowing them the discretion to reduce Council Tax for both individuals and groups of people.

Chapter Fifteen: Health benefits

Health Benefits provide help with the following costs:

- prescriptions
- dental treatment
- sight tests and glasses
- milk and vitamins and healthy food vouchers
- wigs and fabric supports
- hospital travel costs.

Who is entitled?

Maximum, passported help is available if you receive a qualifying benefit. This is one of the following:

- Income Support, or if your income exceeds Income Support requirements by up to 50% of the charge
- the guarantee element of Pension Credit
- Income-Based Jobseeker's Allowance
- if you receive Child Tax Credit or Child Tax and Working Tax Credits or Working Tax Credit with a disability element and with a gross income less than £14,600 pa
- if you are an asylum seeker supported by the Home Office's National Asylum Support Service

If you do not have passported entitlement you can claim on grounds of low income if you also have savings below £8,000 (or £12,000 if over 60 or £20,000 if in residential care). You claim by completing an HC1 form, available from GPs' surgeries, chemists, Post Offices and DWP offices. Awards last for six months, after which it is necessary to re-claim. It is also possible to claim a refund of health costs if a claim is made within three months of purchase. In addition, full help with health costs is also available to other specified groups (see below as these vary slightly).

Prescriptions

Automatic exemption from prescription charges is available to if you are:

- receiving a qualifying benefit (see above)
- aged 60 or over
- under 16, or 19 if still in full time non-advanced education
- under 25 in Wales
- pregnant or have had a baby in the past year
- receiving a War Disablement Pension (but only for treating the pensionable injury/disease)
- a 16 or 17 year old care leaver
- an asylum seeker and dependants supported by the Home Office or
- suffering from one of the following conditions:
  - a continuing physical disability which prevents you from going out without the help of another person

- permanent fistula (including caecostomy, colostomy, laryngostomy or ileostomy) requiring continuous surgical dressing or an appliance
- epilepsy requiring continuous anti-convulsive therapy
- diabetes mellitus except when treated by diet alone
- myxoedema or other conditions which require supplemental thyroid hormone
- hypoparathyroidism
- diabetes insipidus or other forms of hypopituitarism
- forms of hypoadrenalism (including Addison's disease) for which specific substitution therapy is essential or
- myasthenia gravis.

Important issues

- it is helpful if doctors provide their patients with form FP92A (EC92A in Scotland) at the time of diagnosis to confirm one of the above conditions. These forms are available at hospitals, chemists and GP's surgeries
- partial help is not available for prescriptions. People either get them free or have to pay full cost
- people can however purchase a prepayment certificate either for four months or one year. The certificate saves money if you will have more than 14 prescriptions in a year or more than five prescriptions in four months. The pre-payment certificate is used like a season ticket whenever prescriptions need to be collected. Apply on form FP95 from chemists or main Post Offices

- many people are unaware that there are free prescriptions available to you if you have a continuing physical disability which prevents you from going out without someone else's help

- proof of entitlement to free prescriptions will be required by the chemist and people have to sign the back of the prescription form to confirm entitlement

- help is not available for items which cannot be prescribed under the National Health Service, nor for private prescriptions (the latter will have to be paid for at the full commercial cost without any National Health Service subsidy)

- it has been estimated that over one million families are entitled to free prescriptions under the Tax Credit arrangements.

Dental treatment

Maximum, passported help with dental treatment is available if you are:

- receiving a qualifying benefit

- under 18 or 19 if still in full time non-advanced education

- under 25 in Wales

- pregnant or have had a baby in the past year

- War Disablement Pensioners (if your pensionable disability requires dental treatment)

- a 16 or 17 year old care leaver

- an asylum seeker or dependants supported by the Home Office

- aged 60 or over in Wales

Partial help is available if you don't qualify above but do qualify under the low income scheme.

Important issues

- help is only available for NHS treatment. People should check with their dentist before starting treatment as not all dentists offer care under the NHS.

Sight tests and glasses

Free eye tests are available if you are:

- receiving a qualifying benefit
- aged 60 or over
- under 16 or 19 if in full-time, non-advanced education
- registered blind or partially sighted
- prescribed complex lenses
- suffering from diabetes or glaucoma
- aged 40 or over and have a close relative with glaucoma
- a hospital eye service patient
- War Disablement Pensioners if the pensionable condition requires eye tests or glasses or
- a 16 or 17 year old care leaver

In addition to help with sight tests, you can also get vouchers towards the cost of glasses if you:

- receive a qualifying benefit

- qualify under the low income scheme or
- are a War Disablement Pensioner.

Important issues

- vouchers for glasses should cover the cost of a basic pair of glasses but it can be difficult to find glasses within the voucher's value. Some people choose to pay extra with a voucher to buy glasses of their choice. Vouchers cannot be used towards the cost of contact lenses
- you should ask for a glasses voucher when you have an eye test
- it is possible to claim a refund of optical costs if a claim is made within three months.

Healthy Start Scheme

The scheme is new from late 2004/early 2005 and it will provide help with a wide range of health foods (liquid milk, dried infant milk, fresh fruit or vegetables) by providing vouchers worth £2.60 per week (or £5.80 if they have a child under one). It replaces the old milk tokens scheme which is still running till then and which provides tokens to meet the cost of a pint of milk a day. You will qualify if you:

- are aged under 18 and are pregnant (you do not qualify automatically for milk tokens, only the groups below do)
- receive Income Support or Income-Based Jobseeker's Allowance, or have up to £13,480 relevant income for Tax Credits and if you or your partner also:
- are pregnant (need to have application form endorsed by a health professional)
- have a child under 5

- have a disabled child aged 5-16 who cannot go to school because of his/her disability.

Important issues

- not all shops or milk deliverers accept vouchers
- awareness of the new scheme will be low in the early days.

Wigs and fabric supports

Free wigs (e.g. for people being treated by chemotherapy) and fabric supports are available if you are:

- receiving a qualifying benefit
- under 16, or under 19 if still in full-time non-advanced education
- a War Disablement Pensioner
- a hospital in-patient.

Hospital travel costs

Help with travel costs to hospital or clinics for NHS treatment (including out-patient treatment) is available if you:

- receive a qualifying benefit or help under the low income scheme
- are a War Disablement Pensioner (if you need to have treatment for your pensionable disability)
- attend a sexual health clinic.

If you are having treatment, you should ask for help with the travel costs to and from hospital from the hospital receptionist or hospital fares officer. However, it is not uncommon for there to be confusion about who qualifies and who is responsible for payment. NHS provider units (usually hospitals) are responsible for publicity and for having 24 hour reimbursement arrangements.

If you are not able to get to the hospital on your own (e.g. you are a child or are infirm) and you qualify for assistance with your travel costs, you may also get help towards the fares of your companion.

Help towards the cost of travel is usually based on the cost of second class public transport but it can be paid towards the cost of petrol and car parking (including parking on hospital premises) if someone has travelled by car, but only up to an amount equivalent to the cost of public transport. However, taxi fares or the cost of private car fuel and car parking (without a public transport equivalent maximum reimbursement) can be paid if you are unable to use public transport because of a physical disability or no public transport is available for the journey.

Important issues

- if you receive Income Support or Income-Based Jobseeker's Allowance or Pension Credit and visit someone in hospital, you may be eligible for help with fares from the Social Fund

- the clinic or hospital may be private or on a GP's premises as long as the treatment received is paid for by the NHS. It is also possible to get help with the cost of travel abroad if this is for NHS funded treatment

- proof of your travel costs, and that you are on a qualifying benefit, need to be provided to the hospital receptionist or fares office. You will normally be asked to show an award letter from the DWP, but should still claim if evidence is not to hand as this can be sent later

- as with other health costs, if you are neither on the low income scheme nor a qualifying benefit you can get a claim form at the hospital and send off the claim when you return home
- hospital treatment includes ante-natal clinics and day centres on hospital premises
- if you are sent home as part of your hospital treatment or for the hospital's convenience, the hospital should meet the travel costs as part of the treatment costs and not under the travel to hospital scheme
- where the hospital or clinic does not have facilities to refund the fares, the NHS Trust, Primary Care Trust, Health Board or GP should be able to do so
- there is no help available with subsistence or incidental costs on journeys.

Some hospitals have charitable funds which can help.

Chapter Sixteen: Social Fund

The Social Fund exists to help people with intermittent expenses, which can't be met from weekly benefits.

The Social Fund has two parts:

- Regulated and
- Discretionary.

Regulated Social Fund

The Regulated Social Fund is so called because it has rights contained in legislation (regulations), has no budget limit, and there is a right of appeal to an Independent Tribunal if payments are refused.

Payments from the regulated Social Fund are:

- Sure Start Maternity Grant
- Funeral Expenses
- Cold Weather Payments.

Sure Start Maternity Grant

Who is entitled?

You must be receiving one of the following qualifying benefits:

- Income Support
- Income-Based Jobseeker's Allowance

- Tax Credits (but only if at a rate higher than the family element or if a disability or severe disability element is included)

- Pension Credit.

And you must also:

- be expecting a baby in the next 11 weeks or have given birth within the last 3 months, (or are adopting a baby under 12 months old) and

- have confirmation that you have received advice from a health professional (e.g. doctor, health visitor or midwife) about the health and welfare of having a baby.

The Grant is a lump sum of £500 per child and it does not have to be repaid. It is not affected by any capital you have.

How to claim

Claims should be made on form SF100, available from Jobcentre Plus offices, the DWP website and antenatal clinics. If claiming before the baby is born, a maternity certificate (MAT B1), or similar evidence of pregnancy, is required from a doctor, health visitor or midwife and should be enclosed with the SF100 form. The health professional signs the back of the SF100 form to confirm that advice has been given. If claiming after the baby is born, a birth or adoption certificate should be sent with the claim form.

Important issues

- the requirement to show proof of having received advice from a health professional may prevent some people from claiming where a choice has been made not to involve a health professional

- the amount of the grant has been massively increased in recent years but some parents may not be aware of this, especially those on Tax Credits

Cold Weather Payments

Cold Weather Payments help pay for heating costs when the weather is very cold.

You qualify automatically for cold weather payments if:

- you live in a postcode area where a period of cold weather has been forecast or recorded. This is when the average temperature has been at or below 0° Centigrade for at least 7 days and
- you are entitled to Pension Credit, Income Support or Income-Based Jobseeker's Allowance for at least one day during the period of cold weather and
- you also receive at least one of the following premiums in your Income Support or Income-Based Jobseeker's Allowance:
- disability premium
- severe disability premium
- disabled child premium or
- you have a child under 5 years old.

How to claim

There is no need to make a claim as the DWP will automatically assess who is entitled when the cold weather trigger point is reached for an area. The DWP receives data from meteorological stations which inform them when the weather is cold enough.

Cold Weather Payments are in addition to Winter Fuel Payments for those aged 60 plus.

Funeral Payments

These grants are given to help pay for a funeral. They do not have to be paid back, but the cost may be recouped from the estate of the deceased person.

Who is entitled?

If you take responsibility for a funeral, you must be a close relative or close friend of the deceased and you must also receive one of the following benefits on the day of the claim:

- Income Support
- Pension Credit
- Income-Based Jobseeker's Allowance
- Housing Benefit
- Council Tax Benefit
- Tax Credit (but only if at a rate higher than the family element or if a disability element is included).

You must also meet the following rules:

- the deceased must have been ordinarily resident in the UK when they died
- the funeral must take place in the UK
- a claim is made within three months of the funeral
- you must accept legal responsibility for the cost of the funeral and be treated as responsible by the DWP.

If the deceased or the person who has to pay for the funeral is a worker (or member of a worker's family) from a country in the European Economic Area, different rules apply. A grant can be claimed for the cost of a funeral which takes place outside the UK. However, the cost of transporting the body cannot be claimed and the normal limits on costs still apply (see below).

The DWP can treat someone as responsible for the funeral if they were one of the following:

- partner of the deceased or if
- the deceased had no partner and the person claiming or their partner was an immediate family member, close relative or close friend, and it is reasonable for them to take responsibility for the funeral
- immediate family member, means a parent, son or daughter. Close relative, means a parent, parent-in-law, step-parent, son, son-in-law, stepson, stepson-in-law, daughter, daughter-in-law, stepdaughter, stepdaughter-in-law, brother, brother-in-law, sister or sister-in-law.

However, a close relative or close friend can't receive help with the funeral costs if the deceased had a partner or there is a parent, son or daughter of the deceased who does not receive a qualifying benefit (there are some additional exceptions to this rule).

The payment will cover:

- a maximum of £700 towards the cost of the Funeral Director's fees, or £120 if the funeral has been partly paid for by a pre-paid funeral plan or similar and
- the cost of a new burial plot and burial costs or
- the cost of a cremation fee including medical certificates and

- any doctor's fee for the removal of a heart pacemaker or
- up to £20 if removed by the funeral directors.

Also:

- the cost of any documents to release the deceased's assets and
- any excess transport costs over 50 miles where it has been necessary to transport the deceased within the UK and
- the reasonable cost of one return journey within the UK, for the responsible person to either arrange or attend the funeral.

The following will all be deducted from the grant:

- any assets of the deceased which are available without probate or letters of administration
- any payments received because of the death, e.g. from an insurance policy, occupational pension scheme, burial club or similar scheme
- any contributions towards the funeral costs, from charities or relatives
- any funeral grant paid by the Government to a war disablement pensioner
- arrears of the deceased's social security benefit which have been paid to the next of kin
- any amount payable from a pre-paid funeral plan where the plan was not fully paid before the person died.

The DWP can ask for repayment of the grant when the deceased's estate has been settled. Personal possessions left to relatives and the value of a house occupied by the deceased's partner will not count as part of the estate.

How to claim

Complete form SF200, from a DWP office, registry office or funeral director.

Important issues

- people should tell the funeral director that they are applying for a Social Fund funeral payment so that arrangements can be made in line with the allowable costs. Many funeral directors now offer funeral packages within Social Fund grant limits

- the deceased does not need to have been receiving a qualifying benefit

- the complexity and restrictive nature of the rules mean that it is best to clarify responsibility and entitlement before arranging a funeral – though this is about the last thing on one's mind in such circumstances

Discretionary Social Fund

The Discretionary Social Fund has three types of payment:

- Community Care Grants

- Crisis Loans

- Budgeting Loans.

Because it is discretionary, there are not clear rules of entitlement, each local DWP office has a fixed (and small, despite recent increases) budget and there is no right of appeal to an Independent Tribunal. In order to manage expenditure, local offices set priorities within the bounds of national guidance. Research has shown that there is little difference between those whose applications succeed and those whose applications fail. There is particular concern about the erratic nature of Social Fund awards and the hardship caused by loan repayments.

Community Care Grants

You must be receiving Pension Credit, Income Support or Income-Based Jobseeker's Allowance or be likely to be within the following fortnight. Any grant is reduced by the amount of capital over £500 which the person or their partner has (£1000 if they or their partner are 60 or over).

The grant must be needed for one or more of the following purposes:

- to help you or member of your family to (re)establish themselves in the community after leaving institutional or residential care (e.g. hospital, prison, hostel, supported lodgings, care homes and foster care)
- to help someone remain in the community rather then enter institutional or residential care
- to ease exceptional pressure on you and your family
- to allow you or your partner to care for a prisoner or young offender who has been released on a temporary licence
- to help you to set up home as part of a planned programme of resettlement after being homeless
- to help with travel costs (including reasonable, overnight accommodation costs) to visit someone in hospital/residential care.

There is a minimum award of £30 (apart from travel expenses), but no maximum award. Some items are excluded, for example:

work related expenses, distinctive school uniform, medical items, fuel charges, major home improvements or repairs and telephone costs.

Important issues

- applications for Community Care Grants often need to be supported with medical or other evidence, e.g. if someone needs a new bed because of incontinence
- it is important to show how a need is linked to the eligibility criteria for a grant and how a grant will address this
- a family may be experiencing exceptional pressure because it is coping with a disability, ill health, anxiety, depression, relationship breakdown or child care difficulties. There is not a set list and it is not necessary, as a matter of law, to have social work verification or support
- pressures or feelings experienced by children are relevant, for example shame, bullying, discomfort or health risks arising from lack of clothes or facilities in the home
- an effective letter of support from someone who has first hand experience of the circumstances and living conditions will always help the application
- people apply specifically for a Community Care Grant, Crisis Loan or Budgeting Loan, so they may receive more than one payment. However, if they apply for a loan and a loan is awarded, they may be refused a grant on the grounds that the need has been met
- people apply on form SF300 from Jobcentre Plus offices.

Crisis Loans (repayable)

Crisis Loans are intended to be for expenses in an emergency, or because of a disaster.

The person does not have to be on a qualifying benefit but must be aged at least 16. However, the loan must be the only means by which serious risk or damage to the health and safety of the person claiming or a member of their family can be prevented. A loan can be refused if someone does not have the means to repay and it will be limited to what is felt to be repayable.

Crisis Loans are also available to pay for rent in advance on property rented from a private landlord, without showing there is an emergency, disaster or risk to health or safety if a Community Care Grant has been awarded following a stay in institutional or residential care.

Important issues

- supporting evidence may be needed to support a claim where there is serious risk to health or safety
- you must not be discouraged from applying by DWP officials (particularly because not all the facts may be apparent when someone enquires about a Loan). A written decision must also be issued
- you should not be given onerous conditions to satisfy by DWP officials – for example producing receipts for expenditure to show they are destitute
- you should not be told by DWP officials to take out credit nor to ask charities, friends and relatives for money
- if you are subject to a Jobseeker's Allowance sanction who are not getting hardship payments are only able to have a Crisis Loan for items needed for cooking or heating or disaster related expenses during the first two weeks (or the whole period if it is a New Deal or work focussed interview sanction). Seek independent advice in all such cases
- other people who are excluded are people subject to immigration control

- you can apply by phone or on form SF401 from Jobcentre Plus offices.

Budgeting Loans (repayable)

Budgeting Loans are interest-free and awarded for expenses which are difficult to pay out of weekly benefit. However, repayments can take up to a quarter of people's benefit and may continue for a considerable time (even if they go off benefit) thus causing hardship.

Loans are available for the following:

- furniture and household equipment
- clothing and footwear
- rent in advance and/or removal expenses to secure new accommodation
- improvement, maintenance and security of the home
- travelling expenses
- expenses for entering or re-entering work
- Hire Purchase and other debts (for expenses associated with all the above areas).

The amount of loan is based on a calculation involving the purchase, how long you have been on benefit and the amount left in the local Social Fund budget.

To receive a Budgeting Loan you must be receiving Pension Credit, Income Support or Income-Based Jobseeker's Allowance and you and/or partner must have been receiving one of these benefits for 26 weeks before the date when the loan application is decided (but ignoring breaks of 28 days or less).

Important issues

- an application for a Budgeting Loan will not be treated as an application for a Community Care Grant. Separate applications must be made

- there is widespread concern about the dominance of loans in the Social Fund and also about other deficiencies with the Fund. It is always better to apply for a Community Care Grant rather than a loan – don't be put off by DWP officials

- Budgeting Loans are applied for on form SF500 from Jobcentre Plus offices

- weekly repayments are usually deducted from Income Support or Income-Based Jobseeker's Allowance. They can also be taken from other benefits and if someone leaves Income Support (for example, they get a job) the DWP will ask for repayment to continue. The DWP also employs private debt collection companies to pursue old unpaid loans

- the repayments should take account of other commitments including any existing loans. The amount deducted will generally be between 5% - 15%, or up to a maximum 25% of weekly benefit (though the government has announced that it wishes to change the maximum repayment rate). Repayments can be increased if circumstances change. Up to three repayment options will be offered with different amounts over a period of up to 78 weeks

- repayments can be rescheduled if they are causing difficulty

- legally, it is possible to have recovery of a loan completely written off but DWP officials will often refuse to do this, or even deny it is possible. Specialist welfare rights help will be needed. Loan write-offs are most likely in the more extreme circumstances such as serious ill-health or personal circumstances, admission to long term care or prison, or if recovery of a loan would be expensive or complex

- unsatisfactory loan and grant decisions can be challenged by a review process. The first stage is an internal review then the person can ask for a review by a Social Fund Inspector. This is one of the reasons why it is important that DWP officials issue formal written decisions so the system then records that a decision has been made, opening up review rights.

Chapter Seventeen: Education benefits

There is a range of benefits to help with education costs. They are not part of the social security system but can make a significant difference to households on a low income.

Free school meals

Free school meals are available for children of families receiving Income Support or Income-Based Jobseeker's Allowance, and in a few other circumstances. They can also be provided to young pupils aged 16 or over who receive one of these benefits themselves even if their parents don't. They are also paid to families and young people who receive support under Part VI of the Immigration and Asylum Act 1999.

Some schools also provide food at Breakfast Clubs and this should also be free to children entitled to free school meals.

From April 2003, free school meal entitlement was extended to children of parents who receive Child Tax Credit, but who are not entitled to a Working Tax Credit, and whose annual income (as assessed by The Inland Revenue) does not exceed £13,480.

School clothing grants

Local education authorities provide a variety of help with school clothing. The range and amount of help varies from area to area and information should be sought locally. Help is usually targeted at those on means-tested benefits. School clothing grants should not count as income or capital for means-tested benefits. A need for school clothing which is not a distinctive school uniform may qualify for a Social Fund Community Care Grant.

Education Maintenance Allowances (EMAs)

A national EMA scheme is being introduced from September 2004 which will pay a grant to young people who stay in education after school leaving age (16+). The amount paid depends on parental income which is assessed using Tax Credit rules.

Parental income	EMA
Up to £19,630 pa	£30 per week
£19,631 - £24,030 pa	£20 per week
£24,031 -£30,000 pa	£10 per week

For more details phone 080 810 16219

Care to Learn?

Care to Learn? is a new government scheme to help with childcare costs for young parents aged 16 to 18 who are in education or work-based training. For more information telephone 0161 234 7269 (advisers and childcare providers) or 0845 600 2809 (young parents).

Part Two: Help with finding work

Neil Bateman, Chris Brace,
Abena Dadze-Arthur, Mark Morrin,
Donnia Reafat and Will Somerville

Chapter Eighteen: Work Focused Interviews (WFIs)

What are they?

Work Focused Interviews (WFIs) are designed to help people overcome their barriers to work. They require people aged under 60 making a new or repeat claim for certain benefits and who are working less than 16 hours a week, including Incapacity Benefit (but not Disability Living Allowance nor Attendance Allowance), to attend an interview with a personal adviser to talk to them about their work options. If you attend a compulsory interview, you do not have to accept any suggested work or training.

The interviews are conducted at a Jobcentre Plus office and:

- the personal adviser offers help with education, training or getting work, and will discuss whether work might be a possibility

- further mandatory interviews are held at certain 'trigger points'

- the WFI should not involve forcing you into work

- if you do not attend, you might not get your benefits

- in some circumstances, the interviews can be deferred or waived.

A WFI can be waived completely if it would 'not be of assistance' or it would 'not be appropriate'. A WFI can also be deferred to a later date if it is reasonable in your circumstances.

Background

WFIs were introduced in October 2001 as part of a new process for Jobcentre Plus. As well as the WFI, Jobcentre Plus altered the way in which a claim to benefit is made by introducing:

- contact centres – to allow you to claim by phone
- financial advisers – to discuss your claim form before the WFI.

Jobcentre Plus offices are being opened nationally on a rolling programme which will be completed in 2006. Until this time, some areas may not provide a WFI service. This chapter explains the new procedure for claiming benefit in Jobcentre Plus offices.

Things to remember:

1. they are mandatory when you make a claim for certain benefits – your claim won't be processed until you have had an interview (unless it is waived or deferred).
2. you then have more mandatory interviews later on called 'trigger interviews' (especially in the Pathways to Work pilot areas for those on Incapacity Benefit).
3. you can have contact with the Jobcentre Plus office in between, but this is voluntary.
4. they offer a wide range of help to suit your needs.

Aims of the Work Focused Interview

WFIs have been introduced as part of the Government's aim to offer assistance to anyone who is thinking about work.

The main aims of WFIs are:

- to encourage you to see work as a realistic option, where this is appropriate
- to help you build on your skills and potential
- to help you tackle any obstacles to work
- to offer you ongoing support.

Who needs to take part?

It is compulsory to take part in a WFI to receive certain working age benefits. This only applies to new claims after 22 October 2001. In certain circumstances, the interview might be deferred. In exceptional circumstances you might not have to attend at all (see below and page 153 'Waiver'). For other benefits, you can volunteer to attend a WFI.

Do you have to attend a Work Focused Interview?

Answer the following questions to find out.

Question 1 – Age Are you of working age (from 16* to 59)?	YES	NO
Question 2 – Work Are you not working, or working less than 16 hours a week on average?	YES	NO
Question 3 – Benefits Are you or your partner making a new or repeat claim for Incapacity Benefit, residual Severe Disablement Allowance, Carer's Allowance, Income Support or Bereavement Benefits (except Bereavement Payment)?	YES	NO
Question 4 – Where you live Do you live in a WFI area?	YES	NO
If you answered YES to every question, then you probably do have to attend a WFI* If you answered NO to any of the questions, then you do not have to attend a WFI		

* If you are 16 or 17, you have to attend a Learning Focused Interview rather than a WFI

If you are claiming Industrial Injury Disablement Benefit (IIDB), you can choose to have a WFI, but you do not have to have one. If you are between 60 and 65, you do not have to attend a WFI, but you can choose to.

If you are asked to a WFI, you have to attend, unless it is decided that your interview can be waived or deferred until a later date. If you do not attend, this can affect your benefits. You can also lose benefit if you do not take part in the interview by providing certain information when you are asked (see page 156).

Arranging the Work Focused Interview

If you are in a Jobcentre Plus area you should speak to someone at the Jobcentre Plus contact centre to arrange your interview. You can find the number in the phone book, or from the Jobcentre Plus office. You can call the contact centre from the Jobcentre Plus office for no cost.

When you phone the contact centre the person you are speaking to will need quite a lot of information from you, so you should be prepared for a call lasting about 20 minutes. They will take your details and ask what you want to claim. They will also send you claim forms to complete and take to your WFI. If you are interested they might even look for jobs for you over the phone.

When you speak to the contact centre, they will decide whether you need to attend a WFI. If you do need to attend a WFI, they will make arrangements for this. They should try to ensure that the interview is within the next four working days, and in the most convenient Jobcentre Plus office for you. You will not receive benefit until you have attended the WFI, unless it is waived or deferred. If you have no money and ask for early payment of benefit, they should try to book you a WFI immediately. If this is not possible, they might be able to arrange an interim payment, or refer you to the Social Fund for a crisis loan (See chapter 16).

You should be given or sent a letter telling you the date, time and place of your WFI, along with the name of the adviser you will be seeing. You should also receive a leaflet telling you about WFIs.

Getting someone to help you

You can get someone else to phone the contact centre for you; they can also attend the WFI with you. This might be a relative, welfare rights adviser, social worker or someone else. If they do phone the contact centre for you, they will need to have access to a lot of information about you and your situation, as they will be asked various questions over the phone to help decide which benefits you should be claiming, whether a WFI is appropriate and which personal adviser is best placed to help you.

If you would like someone to come with you to the WFI, you should tell the contact centre so this can be sorted out before the WFI takes place. You will need to give consent. The adviser would ideally like written consent from you, but they can accept your verbal consent.

In some cases, the adviser may think it appropriate for the third party to act on your behalf. If you agree that this would be a good idea, they should take steps to arrange this.

At the interview, the adviser should check the personal details of the third party to confirm that they have been appointed to act on your behalf.

What happens at your Work Focused Interview?

When you first attend you will be seen by a financial assessor who will cover the details of your benefit claim. This meeting will take about twenty minutes and will include:

1. Identity Check

The financial assessor will ask you some questions to make sure that you are who you say you are. This is to avoid fraud, and make sure they are not discussing confidential information with the wrong person. They might ask your address or for details of previous benefit claims.

2. Benefit Claim

You will have been issued with the benefit claim forms and asked to bring in evidence to support your claim. The financial assessor will go through the forms you have filled in and check the evidence to make sure that everything is in order. They will discuss the claim with you. You may also ask any questions or raise any concerns you have about your benefit claims.

Once your benefit claim is sorted, the personal adviser will take over the meeting.

The interview

The interview should usually last about 40 minutes. There are a number of things the adviser has to check with you, and information they have to collect. The first interview informs you about the support Jobcentre Plus can offer. The adviser should try to take account of your individual situation when considering what advice to give you. They should try to put you at ease and encourage you.

The purpose of the WFI is to encourage you to take steps to find work, whilst being sensitive to your individual needs and circumstances. They cannot force you to accept work that you are not ready or able to do. The contents of the interview will be as follows:

1. Ethnicity

The adviser might ask you to fill in a leaflet about your ethnicity, if they do not already have this information. This is to help them keep accurate records of who they give assistance to. You do not have to fill this in if you do not want to.

2. Explanation of the Work Focused Interview

Your adviser should provide an explanation of the WFI process, including:

- their role – that they are there to work with you to achieve your job goals
- purpose of the WFI – to tell you what help is available and to help you find work
- what you have to do – that you have to attend and take part in this interview, and further interviews at least every three years
- support from adviser – that you can expect specialist support, and that you can contact them if there is anything you want to discuss about work or training
- benefit queries – that you need to speak to the financial assessor for any benefit queries.

3. Discussion of your circumstances and goals

Your adviser should discuss what your job goals are, if any, along with your current skills, strengths and abilities. This might cover questions about your qualifications, work history, hobbies, salary expectations and personal circumstances.

The adviser should help you work out any barriers to achieving these goals, for example lack of childcare, need for more training and how these could be overcome. This might involve ongoing support, referral to specialist provision, or training and education.

Participating satisfactorily

If you are asked, you must provide answers on:

- if you have a medical condition, how this affects your ability to work
- your education
- your past employment history
- other work skills you have acquired or vocational training you have done
- whether you are currently doing any unpaid or paid work
- whether you have caring responsibilities.

These questions help personal advisers to work out what you can do. If you are asked a question more than once, and have already answered it, you do not have to answer it again.

If you do not answer all of the questions, you are likely to be deemed as not participating, and your claim may not be processed. This requirement applies to initial WFIs and 'trigger point' interviews.

The personal adviser will consider if you had good reason for not answering the question(s). If it is decided that you did not have a good reason the adviser will explain to you the effect that this will have on your benefit claim.

4. Help and support offered

If the adviser feels you are ready to work, they should give you information and advice about what jobs are available. They might look on their database for suitable vacancies.

The adviser may do a better-off in-work calculation and advise you about in-work benefits.

The adviser may try to encourage you to take up an offer of further help in moving towards work. It is up to you if you want to do this. You will be given the option to have further meetings to discuss work or training. You might be eligible for:

- New Deal for Disabled People (see Chapter 19)
- interviews with a Disability Employment Adviser (see page 163)
- more interviews with your WFI personal adviser, offering early access to Jobcentre Plus programmes
- New Deal for Young People, New Deal for 25Plus, New Deal for 50Plus, New Deal for Lone Parents and New Deal for Partners (see page 211).
- Work Based Learning for Adults (see page 217).

The adviser might also offer you help from a specialist voluntary agency, to assist you with any health or caring problems.

If they make an appointment for you to see someone else at a specialist agency, your benefits will not be affected if you decide not to attend. If you do choose to go, your adviser should keep in contact with you to give ongoing assistance.

Depending on your situation, the adviser may offer you in-work support. If you start work but are then considering giving up your job, you can contact your WFI adviser and they may be able to help. You might receive:

- support or mentoring if you have recently started work
- help with jobsearch if you wish to change jobs
- advice about problems encountered after starting work
- access to jobs and/or benefit advice for potential redundancies.

Personal advisers are there to help you, so if you need any specific assistance do not be afraid to ask.

5. Customer Action Plan

The adviser will encourage you to fill in a Customer Action Plan to record what actions you can take towards training or work. The Customer Action Plan sets out clearly the actions which help you to move towards work. This is optional and you do not have to complete it or sign it unless you would like to. It is intended to give structure to subsequent interviews, and help you plan for the future.

6. Arranging further contact

If you and your adviser decide that you would benefit from further contact, you will agree a date for a further interview. This might be with the WFI adviser, or with a different adviser, for example a New Deal personal adviser. Further interviews may be face to face or over the phone. If you do not attend an agreed further interview, it will not affect your benefit, but the adviser should contact you to see if you want to arrange another interview.

If you decide that you do not want interviews at the moment, but might be interested in the future, you can agree a suitable future date for you to attend.

If you do not do this, you will have to attend when a 'trigger point' occurs.

If you want to see your adviser again at any point during your claim, you can contact them and arrange another interview.

You should leave the interview with a clear understanding of what has been agreed and of when you will be having further contact. If you do not feel this is clear, ask the adviser for further explanation.

7. Special arrangement

You may be eligible for a home visit or for the interview to be conducted away from the Jobcentre Plus office.

Reasons set out in DWP guidance for this include:

- poor/non-existent public transport
- severe disability or health problem which makes it difficult to attend
- substantial difficulties in arranging childcare or other care cover
- attending may endanger your health, for example a violent ex-partner living near to the Jobcentre Plus office.

This list is not exhaustive and decisions will be made on a case-by-case basis.

8. Interpreting

If you need someone to interpret, this should be arranged for you or you can choose to bring a friend or relative if you wish. Arrangements should also be made for communication if you are deaf or have a hearing impairment.

Trigger point interviews

If your claim continues, you will be invited for further interviews at certain trigger points. There are two types of trigger points:

1. Time-bound, i.e. you have to go back for another interview after a certain period of time. This will be three years from date of last WFI or other face to face meeting with personal adviser, and every three years thereafter

2. Life events

- starting or ending part-time work
- if you stay on Incapacity Benefit / Income Support following a Personal Capability Assessment (PCA)
- reaching the age of 18
- caring responsibilities have finished or reduced
- starting or ending a training course arranged by Jobcentre Plus.

If you are called in for a trigger point interview, you have to attend. The aim of these interviews is to make sure that no one is left without help to improve their job prospects. The longest anyone will go before being contacted about another interview is three years.

> If you are on Incapacity Benefit, the WFI has no influence on your medical testing arrangements or exemptions.

Trigger point interviews can be deferred or waived in the same way as the initial WFI.

The trigger point interview will be similar to the initial interview, but will not include a discussion with a financial assessor. The trigger point should only cover any changes since the initial interview. If you have a Customer Action Plan, this should be updated to reflect any changes since your first WFI.

Deferral or Waiver

In some circumstances, the WFI might be deferred until a later date, or you might not have to attend at all. When applying for benefit, you need to mention any reasons that mean you might not be able to attend a WFI, or why you think it might not be appropriate or of help for you at that time. If you do not mention these reasons, you will not necessarily be offered a deferral or waiver.

Deferral

You should be offered a deferral if it would be unreasonable for you to attend a WFI at this point or to take part in a discussion about your future prospects, for example if you have just had a baby. The WFI should not place a great burden on you, as you are not forced into work and can receive a home visit. Therefore, it is expected that most people will be able to attend a WFI.

Every situation will be considered on its own merits and the contact centre will make a decision based on discussions with you. If you ask for the WFI to be deferred and it is not, you cannot appeal against the decision (though you can make a formal complaint or possibly take legal action).

A deferral is only made for short period of time based on individual circumstances and you will be contacted at a later date to arrange the interview as long as you are still claiming. This should be explained to you when the interview is deferred. If it is still inappropriate for you to attend the WFI it can be deferred again.

If your interview is deferred you can still proceed with your benefit claim and start getting benefits. This is provided you agree to attend your WFI at an agreed time in the future. If you do not attend the later WFI, you will be given three chances to attend before you are subject to benefit sanctions.

Waiver

The WFI is waived when it is unlikely to be of any assistance to you for the foreseeable future, for example if you are very severely disabled. The WFI can also be waived if you are claiming for a past period only.

If your interview is waived you should be issued with your claim forms and you can proceed straight away with your benefit claim.

You will still be contacted for trigger point interviews (see page 151). However these will also be waived unless there is a change in your circumstances.

Assistance with costs

Who can get assistance?

Certain people can receive a full refund of their travel costs. You might be eligible if you:

- have a health condition or disability (claiming Incapacity Benefit or Income Support with a disability premium)
- are a lone parent
- are a widow or widower (making a claim for or in receipt of Widows Benefit or Bereavement Benefit)
- are a carer (making a claim for or receiving Carer's Allowance).

What you can get: travel costs

If you fall into one of the groups mentioned above, you should receive full payment of any reasonable travel costs at your WFI. Reasonable travel costs include:

- full cost of public transport to the interview
- car or motorcycle mileage
- full taxi fare if there is no other mode of transport available or if you cannot use other transport for health reasons.

If you fall into one of the groups mentioned above, you can also get a refund for the fares of someone accompanying you if they are there to help.

Childcare costs

You are expected to make arrangements for your child(ren) to be looked after by friends or relatives where possible. If you fall into one of the groups mentioned above, and you have caring responsibilities, you can apply to have childcare costs paid back, but only if you use registered childcare. Some providers are exempt from registration and they can also be claimed for. This includes after school clubs or holiday play schemes run on school premises for children aged eight to ten. Childcare costs will be paid direct to the provider.

You can claim childcare until your child is 15, or 16 if they receive Disability Living Allowance or are registered blind. Childcare costs will be paid directly to the childcare provider after you have been to the interview.

What happens if I do not attend or take part?

You have to attend and take part in the initial WFI and in further trigger point interviews or your benefit may be reduced.

If you need to change the time or date of your WFI, you can do so by contacting Jobcentre Plus before the interview. A further interview will then be arranged.

If you are late for an interview or make contact after the time of the interview has passed, you may be treated as having failed to attend.

If you fail to attend an interview you will be contacted to find out why and to remind you of the importance of attending. If you cannot be reached by telephone a letter will be issued. This gives you five days to contact Jobcentre Plus to rebook the interview. If you do not contact Jobcentre Plus within the five day period, your benefit will probably be affected (benefit will not be paid if it is an initial WFI and it will be reduced if it is a trigger point interview).

Each case is considered on its own merits, but you may be required to show just cause for having missed a WFI. The key thing to remember is that you need to contact the adviser as soon as you know you are unable to make an appointment or as soon as you are told you have missed one.

If you have mental health problems which Jobcentre Plus are aware of, and are claiming Income Support, Incapacity Benefit or Severe Disablement Allowance, then the adviser must consult a mental health specialist where available before making any decision about your claim.

Stopping or reducing your benefit

Failure to attend or participate in a WFI without a good reason will lead to your benefit being stopped or reduced. You then have an opportunity to offer a reason for not attending or participating. You have a month after the decision was first made to ask for reconsideration of the decision. You also have the right to appeal.

When is your benefit affected?

- when you do not attend or participate satisfactorily in your first WFI, your benefit claim will be cancelled. You can then make a new claim, but you will still be required to attend a WFI. The claim will start from when you make the new claim, not from the date of the original claim, unless you appeal successfully against the decision to cancel the claim

- when you defer your initial WFI but subsequently fail to attend or participate your benefit will be stopped

- when you fail to attend or participate in a trigger point interview your benefit will be reduced.

You will be sent a letter telling you how your benefit will be affected.

Any reduction in benefit will continue until any of the following things happen:

- a reconsideration or appeal is successful
- you take part in the WFI
- you are no longer entitled to the benefit
- you change address to outside the WFI area
- you reach the age of 60.

If your benefit is affected, the adviser may refer your case to Social Services if they feel that your health is at risk, or a child in your family is at risk due to the change in benefit. If this happens they should discuss and agree this with you first, unless they cannot get in touch with you.

Reconsideration

If you ask for reconsideration of the decision, the personal adviser should explain to you why the decision was made in the first place. If you would still like it to be reconsidered, you can then provide any extra evidence to support your case, and the reconsideration will take place.

Appeal

You can also submit an appeal against the decision but you should normally do so within a month of being told that your benefit has been reduced.

Your benefit should not be affected if:

- you volunteered for a WFI without having to do it

- you are 60-65 years old
- you are claiming Maternity Allowance, or Industrial Injury Disablement Benefit without any of the WFI benefits
- you claimed your benefit before 22 October 2001.

Chapter Nineteen: New Deal for Disabled People (NDDP)

A key part of New Labour's welfare to work policies is the active employment programmes that are designed to assist people into work. As a disabled person or someone with health problems, you may be eligible. There is also other provision available that includes other New Deals – see Chapter 24 Other Welfare to Work initiatives.

The latest performance figures from the New Deal for Disabled People report that, in the last quarter of 2003, there were 4,960 job entries. This was 68% of the number of starts in the period. In the year to December 2003, it achieved 17,860 job entries. This was 53% of the number of starts. Over the life of the programme – since July 2001, 28,910 job entries had been recorded by the New Deal for Disabled People. This was 42% of the number of starts. These figures show that, for those volunteering to join the New Deal for Disabled People, an increasing proportion have been moving into work. The take-up of New Deal for Disabled People is, however, disappointing, with only 69,000 starts since July 2001.

What is it?

The New Deal for Disabled People (NDDP) is a Government initiative to help people with an incapacity, illness or disability return to work. It is delivered alongside other initiatives. NDDP Job Brokers will provide help with looking for a job and any support or training that is needed. This help is completely free. It is a voluntary initiative so you can decide whether or not to use it.

Customers can access NDDP directly through Job Brokers, a voluntary NDDP gateway interview or a Work Focused Interview.

The NDDP aims to support customers, who are on a disability or health related benefit, to prepare for and find paid work, and move off benefits into permanent employment.

Who can take part?

Qualifying benefits

To qualify for NDDP you must be in direct receipt of one or more of the following benefits:

- Incapacity Benefit
- Severe Disablement Allowance
- National Insurance credits on the grounds of incapacity (which may be awarded on their own or in addition to payments of income related benefits – Income Support, Housing Benefit, Council Tax Benefit, or War Pension)
- Income Support with a disability premium
- Income Support pending the result of an appeal against disallowance from Incapacity Benefit
- Disability Living Allowance provided you are not in receipt of Jobseeker's Allowance, and you are not in paid work of 16 hours or more per week
- Housing Benefit with a disability premium, provided you are not in receipt of Jobseeker's Allowance, and you are not in paid work of 16 hours or more per week
- Council Tax Benefit with a disability premium, provided you are not in receipt of Jobseeker's Allowance, and you are not in paid work of 16 hours or more per week
- War Pension with an Unemployability Supplement
- Industrial Injuries Disablement Benefit with an Unemployability Supplement

- a benefit equivalent to Incapacity Benefit that has been imported into the UK under the European Community Regulations on the co-ordination of social security and the terms of the European Economic Area Agreement.

If your entitlement to a qualifying benefit ceases then you will usually become ineligible to participate in NDDP. However, where this is as a result of a Personal Capability Assessment, Job Brokers will arrange a formal de-registration date.

Length of incapacity

There is no qualifying length of incapacity. If you are in receipt of one of the qualifying benefits then you can join NDDP.

Age limits

You will need to be aged between 18 and pension age (60/65) to qualify for NDDP.

However, there are exceptions where you may be entitled to participate at the age of 16 or 17, or beyond state retirement pension age.

If you are aged between 16 and 20 and registered with Connexions or the Careers Service whilst in receipt of a qualifying benefit you will be eligible for participation in NDDP.

Programme elements

Introducing New Deal for Disabled People

Jobcentre Plus staff are responsible for dealing with general NDDP enquiries, including informing you about the programme. NDDP information mailings to customers identified as eligible are sent every six weeks and a National Information Letter is posted annually, although you can request to be removed from the mailings.

You can also be informed about NDDP through any Jobcentre Plus intervention including the following Jobcentre Plus interviews:

- NDDP gateway (a voluntary action)
- Jobcentre Plus Work Focused Interview / Work Focused Meeting
- New Deal personal adviser meeting (see chapter 24 for other New Deals).

As part of the interview, advisers must:

- check your eligibility for NDDP
- explain NDDP and what it involves
- offer you information about NDDP Job Broker services in your area
- offer a full list of all local Job Brokers together with any marketing materials
- encourage you to register with an NDDP Job Broker.

If your eligibility cannot be confirmed immediately, you will be advised that you will only be able to participate once entitlement to a qualifying benefit has been established. If you are not eligible for NDDP you will be able to access other relevant Jobcentre Plus services.

Joint Claims

You may be part of a Joint Claim with an exemption from Jobseeker's Allowance requirements because you receive Incapacity Benefit. In these cases, where you participate in NDDP you will retain your exemption.

Information about NDDP Job Brokers

Advisers must inform you about all the Job Brokers in their local area.

Advisers must show total impartiality towards Job Brokers and must therefore leave the choice of Job Broker to you. However, in order for you to make an informed decision as to which Job Broker will best suit your needs, advisers should give an overview of the services available through each individual Job Broker in their local area, including those that provide specialist customer service; this information should be available locally from Job Brokers, or through your NDDP named contact.

Arranging Job Broker Appointments

There is no formal referral to a Job Broker although you should be encouraged to register with one. If you decide there and then which Job Broker you wish to register with, the adviser may contact that Job Broker to arrange an appointment. Job Brokers have a contractual obligation to interview prospective customers within 10 working days of the initial contact.

Customer follow-up and Disability Employment Advisers (DEAs)

Following the interview, and with your agreement, you may be contacted to check whether you have registered with a Job Broker.

If you have decided not to register with a Job Broker, the adviser may consider taking you onto their own caseload or refer you to a Disability Employment Adviser, (also called a DEA), who provide support to disabled people who are having difficulty in getting a job because of their disability, and also to employed people who are concerned about losing their job because of a disability. They also advise on the Job Introduction Scheme (see p166), WORKSTEP (see Chapter 20) and provide information on the two tick 'Positive About Disabled People' symbol (see p236).

NDDP Job Broker services

Jobcentre Plus contracts Job Brokers on a Local Authority area basis to:

- help you understand the NDDP programme and develop a long-term partnership to support you
- help you find and secure paid work by working with employers to match their vacancies with your skills and potential
- help you to remain in paid work.

Job Brokers come from a range of organisations and offer different services. These services may vary from one broker to another and may involve:

- advice about how to get a job
- help matching your skills and abilities to what employers need
- basic training e.g. interview skills
- advice on training
- support when you start work.

There is at least one Job Broker in each Local Authority area, but there is a choice of Job Brokers in most areas.

To receive Job Broker services, you will need to register with a Job Broker of your choice. As you can only register with one Job Broker at a time, you are advised to find out about all the available local Job Brokers before deciding which to register with. You can do this through your nearest Jobcentre Plus.

Job Brokers have access to other Jobcentre Plus services and consequently may refer you to another programme if you meet the eligibility criteria and the recommended programme is appropriate for you. For example, if a Job Broker feels that WORKSTEP (see Chapter 20) would be an appropriate initiative, you may be referred to a Disability Employment Advisor.

Other Jobcentre Plus programmes and services that Job Brokers have access to are :

Programme	Job Broker's contact at Jobcentre Plus
Access to Work	Access to Work Business Centres/Disability Employment Adviser (DEA)
Action Teams	Jobcentre Plus Adviser
Adviser Discretionary Fund	Jobcentre Plus Adviser
Job Grant	Jobcentre Plus Adviser
Job Introduction Scheme	Disability Employment Adviser/Nominated Officer
ND50+ credit and training grant	ND50+ Personal Adviser
Programme Centres	Jobcentre Plus Adviser
Residential Training for Disabled Adults	Disability Employment Adviser (DEA)
Reduced Rail Fares Scheme	NDDP Policy and Performance Team
Training for Work (Scotland)	Jobcentre Plus Adviser
Travel to Interview Scheme	Jobcentre Plus Adviser
Work Based Learning for Adults (England)	Jobcentre Plus Adviser
Work Based Learning for Adults (Wales)	Jobcentre Plus Adviser
Work Preparation	Disability Employment Adviser (DEA)
Work Trials	Jobcentre Plus Adviser

WORKSTEP referrals

NDDP customers cannot access WORKSTEP through Job Broker services. However, if a Job Broker feels that WORKSTEP would be appropriate, they may refer the customer to a Disability Employment Adviser. If the customer is accepted on the WORKSTEP programme, the Job Broker must de-register the customer.

Job Introduction Scheme referrals

If you are about to start a job and you or your employer have concerns about whether the position or job environment will suit you because of your disability, the Job Introduction Scheme can help financially by paying a weekly grant of £75 to the employer for the first 6 weeks. In exceptional circumstances this may be extended to 13 weeks. The job can be full or part time, but must be expected to last for at least 6 months. The grant may be used to help towards your wages or other employment costs, for example training.

If a Job Broker identifies that an NDDP customer may be suitable for the Job Introduction Scheme, they may also refer the customer to a Disability Employment Adviser or other relevant Jobcentre Adviser. In addition Job Brokers may offer you assistance with your eligibility for in-work benefits.

Participation on NDDP

Once you have registered with a job broker you will have regular and direct contact with them regarding your search for work. Job Brokers will work with employers to help find jobs which will suit your needs.

There is no time limit for your participation on NDDP. However, if you feel that the Job Broker that you are working with is not suitable and that you are not progressing towards work you may de-register and then re-register with a different Job Broker.

Leaving the programme

New Deal for Disabled People is a voluntary programme and as such you may choose to leave the initiative at any time.

Jobcentre Plus staff should encourage you to discuss any concerns with the programme or the Job Broker before you de-register.

When you request de-registration, you can either:

- complete and sign an NDDP6 at your local Jobcentre Plus or Job Broker or
- request de-registration in writing.

If you do not wish to receive further information letters about NDDP, you can request that your details are recorded on an NDDP6 opt-out request form, which should be signed by you. This form is available in your local Jobcentre Plus and will ensure that further national NDDP information letters are not issued.

Customer Complaints

If you have any concerns about Job Brokers services, the Jobcentre Plus adviser will be happy to deal with your complaints.

Benefit sanctions

NDDP is a voluntary programme and as such you cannot be mandated to participate in the programme against your will.

As a NDDP participant you are subject to the same rules as all other recipients of incapacity benefits, including linking rules. These are explained in Chapter 4.

Joining the NDDP will not affect your benefit. You will get help and advice before making any decisions that might affect your benefit, for example going on a Work Trial.

Geographical areas covered

NDDP is a national programme available in all Jobcentre Plus areas to eligible customers.

Future changes

NDDP has been extended and is now contracted to run until the end of March 2006.

In the Budget 2004, Chancellor Gordon Brown introduced a package of measures to break down barriers to work, including a key measure for disabled persons. From the beginning of 2005, a job preparation premium of £20 will be piloted for those on incapacity for work benefits who take active steps to return to work.

Contact

To find out more about New Deal for Disabled People:

- call the NDDP Helpline on 0800 137 177 – or if you use a textphone, call 0800 435 550
- look on the New Deal website at www.newdeal.gov.uk/nddp; or
- look on the JobcentrePlus website at www.jobcentreplus.gov.uk; or
- visit your local Jobcentre, Social Security office or Jobcentre Plus office.

Chapter Twenty: WORKSTEP and service providers

Aim

WORKSTEP is the new name for the Government's supported employment programme, and is designed to provide support in jobs for people with disabilities who have more complex barriers to finding and keeping work. With the right help, and where appropriate, people are encouraged to develop and progress to open employment.

WORKSTEP enables individuals to work effectively in a job by identifying their needs and providing the necessary support to fit their requirements.

For many people WORKSTEP is the stepping-stone into full, unsupported employment. Once in employment, individuals have to come off benefits in order to receive the same wage and terms and conditions as their non-disabled colleagues who do the same or similar work.

Eligibility

All eligible people must be disabled, as defined by the Disability Discrimination Act 1995.

If you are eligible a Jobcentre Plus contact, likely to be a Disability Employment Adviser, will be able to refer you to a WORKSTEP service provider. The service provider will be able to create a tailored training plan with you and match you with an appropriate employment opportunity.

To qualify for WORKSTEP you must be in receipt of one of the following benefits, or else fall into one of the following people categories:

- Incapacity Benefit and/or National Insurance Credits (including Severe Disability Allowance and Income Support)

- Jobseeker's Allowance (JSA) and/or National Insurance Credits for six months or more

- JSA and/or National Insurance Credits for less than six months if you were receiving Incapacity Benefit before claiming JSA

- you have been supported by WORKSTEP before and need to return to the programme within two years

- you are currently in work but at serious risk of losing your job as a result of disability, even after your employer has made all reasonable adjustments and considered other available support options

- you are a recent/prospective education leaver who does not fall within the groups above, but for whom there is clear evidence of a need for support in work. Typically you will have stayed in education for an extended period and evidence to support your eligibility may be available, for example, from periods of work experience.

Linking provision acts in the same way as with all JSA claims, i.e. two or more jobseeking periods can be treated as one if they are separated only by:

- a linked period (for any length of time) comprising Incapacity Benefit, Invalid Care Allowance, Maternity Allowance or Training Allowance

- a break in a jobseeker's claim, where the claim is terminated for not more than 12 weeks between any two linked jobseeking periods or

- any length of time spent on jury service.

If you are found to fulfill the eligibility criteria for both StepUP and WORKSTEP, you will be given the opportunity to participate in WORKSTEP if it is assessed that this is the best option. Under these circumstances you will be exempt from StepUP, however if exemption from StepUP is given you cannot then opt out of WORKSTEP.

Participating in WORKSTEP is in any other case entirely voluntary and if necessary you may choose to leave the programme early.

Service Providers and Programme Elements

A service provider works very closely with you and an employer to ensure that your job matches your needs by:

- designing an individual development plan and support package to help you make the most of your potential. This may include job tasters or work experience, access to learning and training, as well as job coaching or training (should this be necessary)
- reviewing your progress regularly and updating your development plan to show how you have grown and gained the skills you need
- working with you and your employer to assist you to progress into mainstream employment and
- working closely with the Disability Employment Adviser at Jobcentre Plus to arrange any other support you may need to assist you into work, for example Access to Work funding.

Jobcentre Plus contracts with over 200 service providers (including local authorities, voluntary organisations and private training companies) to deliver the WORKSTEP programme across the UK.

At present there are 26,000 disabled people participating in WORKSTEP, and four main service providers, Remploy, Scope,

Shaw Trust and Employment Opportunities, that deliver half of all the programming.

Details of these main four and all other service providers are listed below, grouped by geographical location along with a summary of particular services they offer.

Local authorities that participate in WORKSTEP are detailed at the end of each section. Some of them fund and run factories and other employment enterprises in the locality that are specifically geared to the employment of disabled people. They may also find you a job within local authority offices or else place you with an external organisation. You can look at their websites for further details.

Major WORKSTEP providers

Remploy - England, Scotland and Wales

They are the largest employer of disabled people in the UK and the largest single provider of WORKSTEP within Jobcentre Plus. They are also a provider of New Deal for Disabled People.

Remploy was first established in 1946 to provide work for disabled ex-servicemen. Today it employs around 9,000 disabled people - approximately 5,500 are based in a network of 81 factory locations across England, Scotland and Wales. The factories supply half of the top British companies with goods and services. Products include high-tech motor and electronic assemblies, school and college furniture, printing and packaging as well as protective clothing for military and civil use.

As well as employing disabled people to work in Remploy factories, over 3,500 are also assisted into jobs with mainstream host employers. Remploy is funded through revenue generated from its commercial activities and a substantial grant in aid from Government, which was set for 2003/04 at £115 million.

Scope – England and Wales

Scope is a disability organisation in England and Wales whose focus is people with cerebral palsy. Their aim is for disabled people to achieve equality in society where they are as valued and have the same human and civil rights as everyone else.

Scope's Employment Support Services offer a range of employment support through a team of Employment Officers across England (Brighton and Hove, Calderdale, Chester, Devon, London, Middlesbrough, Plymouth, Rotherham), and in North and South Wales (Cwmbran, Sully).

They also run the European Union funded 'Transition to Work' project, work in partnership with young people on the 'Millennium Volunteers' project and run the 'Fast-Track' employment scheme for disabled graduates in conjunction with some of the UK's leading employers.

Shaw Trust – England, Scotland and Wales

A variety of government programmes are used by the trust to assist disabled people in finding and keeping employment. Last year they provided 7,000 employment opportunities for disabled people throughout the UK. Many of their services are tailored to the specific requirements of people with mental ill health, substance misuse problems or learning disabilities.

The main offices are based in London, Worcestershire, Wiltshire, Middlesbrough and Neath. They also have specialist centres, which offer people a variety of pre-employment activities, work-related learning and support for increased independence.

The trust also operates a family of light industry enterprises, which manufacture or finish products for business-to-business markets. Products and services currently include: powder coating services, plastic extruded products, assembly and processing services and making UPVC products. Income generated from commercial activities is reinvested to help sustain the enterprises and to increase social enterprise opportunities.

Employment Opportunities – England, Scotland and Wales

The Charity was founded in 1980 by ten major City of London Employers; The Bank of England, BP, CEGB, IBM, Midland Bank, P&O, Price Waterhouse, Sedgwicks, Stock Exchange and Unilever.

Employment Opportunities is a national charity helping people with disabilities find and retain work. They have 20 centres across England, Scotland and Wales where they provide a wide range of support and advice to employers on disability and employment issues.

Their offices can be found in the following areas; London (Great Portland Street and New Broad Street), Birmingham, Brentwood, Bristol, Bedford, Brighton, Cardiff, Colchester, Edinburgh, South Hampshire, Glasgow, Kingston upon Thames, Leigh-on-Sea, Leicester, Luton, Mersey and Deeside, Newcastle, Reading, Sheffield and Stockport.

London WORKSTEP providers

Action for Blind People – Bermondsey

They are the third largest charity in the UK working with blind and partially sighted people. The charity's Employment Development Team provides support and advice on all aspects of employment in relation to visually impaired people. They also have offices in Carlisle, Liverpool, Middlesborough, Preston, Birmingham and Exeter.

The Team aims to reduce the number of visually impaired people who are unemployed (75% of blind and partially sighted people of working age are unemployed) and increase the number of people who develop a sight problem in work, to keep their jobs.

They also work with the Employment Services, Social Services, local blind societies and employers to further the employment and retention of visually impaired people.

Royal London Society for the Blind - Park Royal

The Royal London Society for the Blind is committed to empowering people with a visual impairment to lead independent lives through the provision of high quality education, training and employment services.

Workbridge is the Employment Service of the Royal London Society for the Blind and is located in London and the Home Counties. The team is specifically geared to support visually impaired people into sustainable and rewarding employment or assist people to retain employment.

Islington Mind - Islington

Islington Mind is the leading mental health charity in England and Wales. If you have experienced mental health problems, the Islington branch can provide you with support in all aspects of employment, including voluntary work, training, pre-vocational counselling, paid work and employment advice and support.

Disability Times Trust - Ealing

The Disability Times Trust centre in Ealing offers practical support about all areas of employment for around 90 people every day. Facilities at the centre include an employment training area with six classrooms, an interactive job search area, a social area and a café.

Tailored programmes operate in sectors such as Graphic Design, Desktop Publishing and Telesales. Work placement, CV writing, interview and telephone techniques, personal development and English language (ESOL) courses are also offered.

Local Authorities

Croydon Borough Council
Brent Borough Council
Ealing Borough Council

Hackney Borough Council
Haringey Borough Council
Havering Borough Council
Hillingdon Borough Council
Hounslow Borough Council
Islington Borough Council
Merton Borough Council
Redbridge Borough Council
Royal Borough of Kingston-Upon-Thames
Richmond upon Thames London Borough Council
Waltham Forest Borough Council
Wandsworth Borough Council

South East WORKSTEP providers

National Society for Epilepsy (NSE) – Chalfont

The National Society for Epilepsy is committed to providing information and support to people with epilepsy. The society helps people with epilepsy, and their employers, find solutions to any practical obstacles arising from their disability within the work place. It offers practical advice and help in a flexible way so that it can be tailored to particular needs.

This may include help with the cost of getting to and from a place of work, help with funding for adaptations or additional equipment, or help providing extra support or communicators within the workplace.

The Royal British Legion Industries (RBLI), also comprising Workwise Employment Services – Aylesford.

Royal British Legion Industries is an independent charity working in partnership with The Royal British Legion and Employment Services. It also works closely with Health and Social Services. Its objectives are to provide care and support for ex-Servicemen and women, and also to provide employment and training for people with disabilities, whether from an ex-Service background or not.

The RBLI also operate under the Workwise brand, and have branches in Kent, Sussex, Essex, Surrey and Newcastle. Some work opportunities also exist within the RBLI manufacturing site at Aylesford, Kent, where the production of pallets, signage and other light assembly work take place. You could also be placed through the RBLI with host organisations around the South East and in the North East of England.

Local Authorities

Brighton & Hove Council
Kent County Council
Isle of Wight County Council
Oxford County Council
Portsmouth City Council
Slough Borough Council
Surrey County Council
Yateley Town Council

East of England WORKSTEP providers

Meridian East – Norwich

The company's main training centre is based in the centre of Norwich, with others centres also operating in Great Yarmouth, Thetford and Kings Lynn. The centres provide up-to-date information technology rooms, practical training areas as well as access to the services of specialist occupational therapists and community nurses. Some of their staff are on long-term secondment from other organisations.

Meridian receives a number of funding sources other than WORKSTEP, including the Department of Health and Social Services, European Social Fund and Norfolk Mental Health (NHS).

The Papworth Trust - Cambridge

The trust operates across Norfolk and Suffolk and last year supported over 220 people in permanent employment with more than 80 host companies through WORKSTEP.

The programme provides people with a disability ongoing support allowing permanent employment in the open job market. For the employer it can provide practical and financial assistance towards employing or retaining a disabled employee. Advice on other schemes, such as Access to Work, is also available.

Local Authorities

Basildon District Council
Bedfordshire County Council
Peterborough City
Norfolk County Council
Essex County Council
Suffolk County Council
Harlow District Council
Watford Borough Council
Norfolk County Council
Peterborough City Council
Suffolk County Council
Southend-on-sea Borough Council
Suffolk County Council
Watford Borough Council

South West WORKSTEP providers

Local Authorities

Bath and North East Somerset County Council
Bournemouth Borough Council
Bristol City Council

Exeter County Council
Cornwall County Council
Cinderford Town Council
Devon County Council
Gloucester City Council
Dorset County Council
Plymouth City Council
Poole Borough Council
Somerset County Council
South Gloucestershire City Council
Swindon Borough Council

North East WORKSTEP providers

City Centre Training – Middlesborough

Most of the training carried out is based in the Tees Valley. They provide a broad range of training which includes work based learning in animal care, engineering, technology and manufacturing, business administration and management, information and communications technology, as well as retail, leisure and health and social care.

Mencap - Rotherham

Mencap works with people with a learning disability, their families and carers. Mencap's Education and Employment Business Unit facilitate the WORKSTEP programme in conjunction with their own 'Pathways' project. They operate throughout England and Wales and offer education, training and employment services to enable people with a learning disability to achieve their goals.

Remploy – (see Major providers)

The Royal British Legion Industries (RBLI) – (see South East providers)

Shaw Project – (see Major providers)

J&J Training – Northumberland

J & J Training Limited is a training provider based centrally in Morpeth and Ashington in Northumberland specialising in confidence and stamina building, assessment of skills and abilities and facilitation of work placement opportunities.

They provide an employment training and rehabilitation service, which includes catering for adults of working age (18 to 65) who have barriers to employment, additional learning needs and who may be disadvantaged.

Local Authorities

South Tyneside Council
Stockton Borough Council
Sunderland City Council
Durham City Council
Durham County Council
Middlesbrough County Council
Newcastle-upon-Tyne City Council
Newcastle-under-Lyme Borough Council
North Tyneside Council
Northumberland County Council

North West WORKSTEP providers

Barrowmore Supported Employment - Chester

Barrowmore are dedicated to including differently abled people into the workforce and customer base of the UK. Their service assists people with disabilities to obtain work and develop their careers.

Cheadle Royal Industries Limited (CRI) - Cheadle

CRI is a registered charity and manufacturer of party hats and novelties, created in 1957 to help support people with learning difficulties and mental health problems into employment.

Oaklea Trust – Kendal

The Oaklea Trust operate across Cumbria, Lancashire, County Durham, Northumbria and Greater Manchester and are a charitable organisation whose sole purpose is to support and assist children and adults with all types disabilities to lead fulfilled lives within their communities.

Scope – Middlesbrough (see Major providers)

Local Authorities

Barrow in Furness Borough Council
Blackburn with Darwen Borough Council
Blackpool Borough Council
Bolton Metropolitan Borough Council
Bury Metropolitan Council
Cheshire County Council
Cumbria County Council
Knowsley Metropolitan Borough Council
Lancashire County Council
Liverpool City Council
Oldham Metropolitan Borough Council
Rochdale Metropolitan Borough Council

Salford City Council
Sefton Metropolitan Borough Council
Stockport Metropolitan Borough Council
Tameside Metropolitan Borough Council
Trafford Metropolitan Borough Council
Wigan Metropolitan Borough Council
Wirral Metropolitan Borough Council

Yorkshire & The Humber WORKSTEP providers

Hull College – Hull

Hull College's Board of Study, Widening Participation, runs the WORKSTEP programme in partnership with the Employment Service, and aims to find participants suitable employment via their industry contacts in the local area.

Mencap – Gateshead (see North East providers)

Shaw Trust – Doncaster (see Major providers)

Local Authorities

Barnsley Metropolitan Borough Council
Bradford Metropolitan Borough Council
Calderdale Metropolitan Borough Council
Doncaster Metropolitan Borough Council
East Riding of Yorkshire District Council
Kingston Upon Hull Metropolitan Borough Council
Kirklees Metropolitan Borough Council
Leeds Metropolitan Borough Council
North Lincolnshire District Council
Sheffield City Council
Wakefield District Council
York City Council

East Midlands WORKSTEP providers

Local Authorities

Nottingham City Council
Derbyshire County Council
East Lindsay District Council
Northamptonshire County Council
Leicester City Council
Leicestershire County Council
Lincolnshire County Council
Northamptonshire County Council
Nottinghamshire County Council

West Midlands WORKSTEP providers

Beacon Employment (BE) - Kidderminster

Beacon Employment was established in 1992 to provide education, training and support for people with learning disabilities to enter employment. They have training centres in Stourport, Kidderminster and Dudley offering training in practical skills such as bricklaying, mechanics and landscaping. Their WORKSTEP programmes cover the Black Country. BE also has contracts with Worcestershire Social Services, Learning and Skills Council, local education authorities, Connexions and other funding organisations.

Carver Training - Wolverhampton

Carver Training is a private training organisation operating locally. They provide training and support employment placements mainly in the areas of business retail, administration and customer services while assisting the individual working towards NVQ level certificates.

Mencap Pathway - Stoke (see North East providers)

Rathbone Community Industry - Wolverhampton

Rathbone CI offers to people with moderate learning difficulties and other special needs, employment preparation, employment searches, independent advice on special education, vocational education and work experience. They also have a main office in Manchester.

Local Authorities

Birmingham County Council
Coventry County Council
Sandwell Metropolitan Borough Council
Warwickshire County Council
Shropshire County Council
Worcestershire County Council
Solihull Metropolitan Borough Council
Stoke City Council
Walsall Metropolitan Borough Council
Warwickshire County Council
Wolverhampton County Council
Wolverhampton City Council
Worcestershire County Council

Wales WORKSTEP providers

Agoriad - Bangor, Pwllheli, Dolgellau

Agoriad exists to facilitate the progression of people with disabilities into work. Its primary activities all focus on helping clients achieve their potential so that they become valued members of the workplace. They offer full training and work search programmes and forge links with local organisations such as leisure centres.

Foothold

Foothold Crochan is a Community Recycling initiative that recycle and reuse materials, furniture and white goods and offer refurbished items to those in need, and reduce the level of waste going to landfill. They also provide skills and training to those in need in occupations such as woodmaking and general warehouse training. The Foothold group is based in Llanelli.

Shaw Trust (see major providers)

RBLI (see South East providers)

Local Authorities

Blaenau Gwent County Borough Council
Cardiff City Council
Carmarthenshire County Council
Ceredigion County Council
Denbighshire County Council
Swansea, City & Council
Newport City Council
Pembrokeshire County Council
Powys County Borough Council
Rhondda Cynon Taff County Borough Council
Swansea City and County Council
Torfaen County and Borough Council
Ynys Mon / Isle of Anglesey County Council

Scotland WORKSTEP providers

Capability Scotland

Capability Scotland offers a range of services that support disabled people into employment. Their employment development offices operate throughout Scotland in Edinburgh, Elgin, Grangemouth, Glasgow, Whitehaugh Centre, Paisley, West Lane Gardens and Johnstone.

Hansel Alliance – Symington, Ayrshire

Hansel Alliance provides work opportunities for employees who require varying levels of support. They currently support approximately 60 people in employment with companies throughout Ayrshire, Glasgow, Argyll and the Isles. They also provide employment opportunities to approximately 30 people within 3 small business initiatives that operate from the Hansel premises in the fields of knitwear, laundry and gardening.

Holywood Trust - Dumfries

The Holywood Trust assists young people (15-25 year olds) resident in Dumfries and Galloway, in South West Scotland, particularly those experiencing mental, physical and social disadvantage.

Momentum - Glasgow

Momentum works in partnership throughout Scotland to enable and empower disabled and excluded people to identify and achieve their goals. They support people to remain active citizens within their own communities, through the provision of mainstream employment and personal support services.

Scottish Association for Mental Health - Glasgow

SAMH operates a range of services across Scotland for people with mental health problems. It also strives to influence public policy as it affects people with mental health problems.

They also run a Therapeutic Earnings Scheme, which allows people to work on a part time basis where it is considered that the employment has therapeutic value in relation to their level of disability.

Wise Group – Glasgow

The Wise Group is a charitable organisation which is dedicated to helping unemployed people back into work. The Wise Group provides training and employment opportunities for unemployed and workless adults throughout Scotland and the North East of England.

The head office and main training facilities are both located in Glasgow. Other offices are in North, South and East Ayrshire, Renfrewshire and East Renfrewshire, East and West Dunbartonshire, Lanarkshire, Dumfries, Inverclyde, Edinburgh, West Lothian, Newcastle and Tees Valley.

Local Authorities

Aberdeen City Council
Aberdeenshire Council
Argyll and Bute Council
Borders Council
Clackmannanshire Council
Dundee City Council
Dumfries and Galloway Council
East Ayrshire Council
East Lothian Council
East Renfrewshire Council
Edinburgh City Council
Falkirk Council
Fife Council
Glasgow City Council
Highland Council
Inverclyde Council
Midlothian Council
Moray Council
North Ayrshire Council
North Lanarkshire Council
Orkney Islands Council
Renfrewshire Council
Shetlands Islands Council
South Ayrshire Council
South Lanarkshire Council
Stirling Council
West Dunbartonshire Council
West Lothian Council
Western Isles Council

Chapter Twenty-one: Pathways to Work Pilots

What are they?

The Pathways to Work Pilots are about the reform of Incapacity Benefit. The reforms aim to help those with a moderate health condition or disabled people get back into work.

The provisions in the pilot areas are for people claiming incapacity benefits as a new or repeat claimant. Existing clients will, however, be able to access any element of the provisions on a voluntary basis.

Programme elements

Customers in the pilot areas have to attend their first Work Focused Interview with a specialist Incapacity Benefit personal adviser. If you are able to go back to work then a Choices package will be offered. The Choices package includes:

- a new credit called the Return to Work Credit (RTWC) of £40 per week. RTWC is available if you have been on Incapacity Benefit for at least 13 weeks and take up a job of 16 hours or more and retain the job for at least five weeks. It is payable for 52 weeks. The earnings from the job should be less than £15,000 a year

- immediate access to the Adviser Discretion Fund (ADF), which is a maximum £300 payment to enable customers in overcoming difficulties when getting a new job (see page 199)

- New Condition Management Programmes, run jointly by local NHS providers and Jobcentre Plus, offering short courses in understanding and managing your health condition

- engagement of other key stakeholders – particularly employers and GPs.

Where are they?

The pilot areas are:

- Bridgend
- Rhondda Cynon Taff
- Derbyshire
- Essex
- East Lancashire
- Gateshead
- South Tyneside
- Somerset
- Refrewshire
- Inverclyde
- Argyll and Bute.

Chapter Twenty-two: Job Retention and Rehabilitation Pilots and Working Neighbourhood Pilots

Job Retention and Rehabilitation Pilots

Aim

The Job Retention and Rehabilitation Pilot (JRRP) was announced in 2000, commenced in April 2003 and is running for two years. JRRP is funded by the Department for Work and Pensions in partnership with the Department of Health and is supported by the Scottish Executive, the Health and Safety Executive and the Welsh Assembly.

The aim of the JRRP is to assess the net impact and relative effectiveness of three different delivery and intervention strategies in preventing job loss following the onset of sickness, injury or disability and how these link with effective outcomes.

It also looks at ways of assisting you in getting back to, and remaining in, work.

External service providers are delivering three distinct areas of interventions, assessing which of the following is more effective in supporting the JRRP aims;

- Group One: a co-ordinated boost to rehabilitation, healthcare and advice services
- Group Two: a co-ordinated boost to workplace interventions
- Group Three: a combination of both work-based support and health care services.

Elements to the programme include service providers drawing up an action plan with you for your return to work that is appropriate to your individual health condition, and according to the intervention group you are put in touch with.

You also work with an individual case manager who keeps in touch with you to assist with and revise your action plan where necessary, organises your appointments for the appropriate treatments and services and for research pilot purposes and monitors your return to work.

As a participant in any of the three pilot groups, your rights to all Jobcentre Plus services, programmes and benefits do not change.

Eligibility

The project is open to employed and self-employed volunteers who are at risk of job loss because they have been absent from work for reasons of ill health, injury or disability for between six and 26 weeks.

If you are interested in volunteering in the pilot areas you will be asked by your Jobcentre Plus contact to get in touch with a national contact centre, and if you are eligible, you will be randomly assigned to one of the three specific research groups as detailed above.

It has been recognised that in particular musculo-skeletal, cardiovascular and mental health conditions account for 60% of all episodes of statutory sick pay that last between six weeks and six months, and so is of significant interest. However, all individuals are eligible to volunteer for the pilots regardless of what their health problem or disability may be.

Where are they?

JRRP is running for two years in six pilot areas across the country and four service providers are delivering them.

JRRP will be running under the following brand names:

- Greater Glasgow (HealthyReturn)
- Teesside (Routeback)
- Tyneside (Routeback)
- Birmingham (WorkCare)
- Sheffield (WorkCare)
- West Kent (WorkCare)

Working Neighbourhood Pilots

Aim

Working Neighbourhood Pilots (WNP) are not directly aimed at those with health or caring issues. However, they are relevant as they have been set up to test a new way of offering intensive support to local residents. This support is focused on overcoming barriers to employment and accessing jobs within travelling distance of where you live. It is to be achieved by ensuring you are offered work-focused contacts throughout your interaction with Jobcentre Plus and that you are provided with in-work support and incentives to help you once you have a job.

The programme is being piloted in 12 of the most deprived neighbourhoods in the country for two years from April 2004.

Eligibility

You are eligible for support if you are:

- claiming Jobseeker's Allowance, Income Support or Incapacity Benefit
- economically inactive, aged 18-60, and resident in the pilot areas. If you are in this second group, joining the pilots is voluntary.

Programme Elements

The support available depends on the benefits you are currently claiming. This support has been based on the recognition that these neighbourhoods often combine high levels of unemployment with widespread employment opportunities nearby.

Incapacity Benefit

More help will be available to ensure that employment opportunities are identified and appropriate help and support discussed and made available.

Partners

If you are getting additional benefits due to your partner, and are claiming Income-Based Jobseeker's Allowance, Income Support, Incapacity Benefit or Severe Disablement Allowance, your partner will also be required to attend Work Focused Interviews.

During these interviews you will agree an Action Plan with your personal adviser. This will identify the steps you need to take to prepare for work or training.

Services are delivered by personal advisers who have access to a discretionary fund. This is to be used to deliver services that best meet the needs of the local community. This flexibility is key to the pilots, and local programmes will be designed in conjunction with the Local Strategic Partnership. This money can be spent on community projects that will help you and other residents overcome the barriers that exist locally and are preventing you from starting work.

In-Work Support

There is funding also available to help you once you have found work. You will receive two lump sum payments, in addition to any other incentives available. The first will be paid to you after you have been in work for 13 weeks, and the second larger payment will be paid to you after you have been in work for 26 weeks.

Geographical Areas

Twelve areas have been selected to be part of this pilot. Based on postcodes, they are selected parts of the following wards (if you live in a neighbouring ward you may also be eligible):

- Glasgow - Parkhead
- Glasgow - Hutchesontown
- Birmingham – Aston
- Newcastle - Byker and Walker
- Hastings - Castle
- Swansea – Penderry
- Great Yarmouth - Central & Northgate
- Knowsley - Northwood
- Wirral - Birkenhead
- Tower Hamlets - East India & Lansbury
- Sheffield - Manor
- Middlesbrough - Thorntree

Jobcentre Plus will deliver the pilots in seven of these areas. If you live in an Employment Zone area, provision will be delivered by the Employment Zone contractor. These are the wards in Birmingham, Tower Hamlets, Glasgow (two pilots) and

Middlesborough. If you live in an Employment Zone area, but do not claim Jobseeker's Allowance, you can choose whether you receive services from the Employment Zone provider or Jobcentre Plus.

Chapter Twenty-three: Financial support for those moving into work

Introduction

People who move from benefits into work may face a loss of income, particularly if they are on means-tested or disability benefits and are moving into low paid work. The benefits system has been much improved in recent years to make it easier for people to move from benefits into work. In particular, Tax Credits are designed to make the transition as positive as possible. It is important to try to ensure that people have access to a better-off calculation (usually with a computer package) before they make decisions about entering work, as an unexpected negative experience can be very damaging. Such a calculation should be available from welfare rights advisers, or local advice centres. Some Jobcentre Plus staff may also carry them out. However, Jobcentre Plus staff have a vested interest in meeting targets for getting people back into work and may not always fully appreciate loss of incidental benefits such as free school meals and prescriptions.

Additional difficulties with moving from welfare to work can be created by delays in Housing and Council Tax administration.

The following is a brief summary of some of the financial help available to help people move into work:

Back to Work Bonus

This helps people take part-time work which may turn into full time work. People receiving Income Support or Income Based Jobseeker's Allowance can build up earnings from part-time work (less than 16 hours a week) while on benefit which is then paid to them as a lump sum of up to £1000 when they move into work of at least 16 hours a week. Half of any earnings above their earnings disregard are counted towards a bonus.

The Bonus can start when someone has been in part time work and on Income Support for at least 91 days and they must enter full time work within 14 days of leaving benefit. It must be claimed within 12 weeks of going off benefit and into full-time work, but will be paid automatically when someone reaches the age of 60 (or state pension age if they receive Jobseeker's Allowance).

The Back to Work Bonus is being phased out from 25 October 2004.

Job Grant

What is it?

A £100 tax-free payment for people entering full-time work (16 hours a week or more). From October 2004, the government plans to increase it to £250 for people with children. It does not count as income or capital for means tested benefits.

Who is it for?

You can claim Job Grant if:

- you are aged 25 or over
- you have received Income Support, Jobseeker's Allowance, Incapacity Benefit, or Severe Disablement Allowance, or a combination of these for at least 52 weeks (if you have been on a New Deal or Employment Zone scheme, it counts towards the 52 weeks providing you were in receipt of Jobseeker's Allowance at the time) and
- the full-time work is expected to last 5 weeks or more.

If you are working part-time and the hours you are working increase to 16 or more, then you may be able to claim Job Grant. Similarly, if your full-time work is self employed, then you may be able to qualify.

However, lone parents are not eligible for Job Grant until October 2004 but may be able to claim the Lone Parent's Benefit Run On (see next page).

If you would like to claim Job Grant, contact your local Jobcentre Plus.

Please note that you are only able to claim one Job Grant during any 52 week period.

Adviser Discretion Fund

The Adviser Discretion Fund is held by personal advisers at Jobcentre Plus. From this fund, they can allocate up to £300 to those on New Deal, and those who have been receiving Jobseeker's Allowance and Income Support for more than six months, to help them overcome any barriers that they may face in looking for or getting work. This may include buying clothes, paying for travel and childcare costs, etc.

If you are unable to afford to buy something that you need to look for or start work, your local Jobcentre Plus personal adviser may be able to help you.

If you are refused help there is no right of appeal to a Tribunal, but you can make a formal complaint or take the matter up with your MP.

Social Fund

The Social Fund is a one-off benefit to pay for a particular need.

There are two parts:

- Regulated Social Fund – this helps you with expenses which arise for a specified reason: maternity expenses, funeral expenses, cold weather payments, and winter fuel payments.
- Discretionary Social Fund – provides grants and loans to meet a variety of other needs such as clothing or furniture.

You will have to meet the criteria such as being in receipt of certain benefits such as Income Support or Income-Based Jobseeker's Allowance. Furthermore, receiving help from the Discretionary Social Fund is notoriously complex and perseverance is crucial. See Chapter 16 for further details.

Travel to Interview Scheme

Payments for interview travel costs and overnight accommodation if an interview is more than an hour's one way travel. The payments are available from Jobcentre Plus for people who have been receiving Jobseeker's Allowance or signing on for National Insurance Credits for at least 13 weeks (though people covered by the New Deals for Partners or Lone Parents may get immediate access). The interview must be for a job of at least 30 hours a week and be expected to last at least a year. People must apply before the interview.

Lone Parent Run On

This will pay two week's Income Support (and two week's Housing Benefit and/or Income Support housing costs) to lone parents who are starting work for at least 16 hours a week in a job which is expected to last at least five weeks if the lone parent:

- received Income Support or Income-Based Jobseeker's Allowance immediately before they start work, and
- have been on Income Support or Income-Based Jobseeker's Allowance for at least 26 weeks continuously, and
- has been a lone parent for at least 26 weeks.

The local Jobcentre Plus office should be told before the lone parent starts work and it does not need to be separately claimed.

Rapid Reclaim

This is designed to help people take temporary work. If they reclaim Jobseeker's Allowance or Income Support within 12 weeks and their circumstances have not changed, they fill in a shorter claim form and their claim is then fast-tracked for a decision to reduce delay and uncertainty.

Housing and Council Tax Benefit Rapid Reclaim

In the same circumstances as Income Support and Jobseeker's Allowance Rapid Reclaim, a shorter claim form (RR1) is completed.

Extended Housing and Council Tax Benefits

This provides for four weeks of maximum Housing and/or Council Tax Benefit when someone on Income Support or Income-Based Jobseeker's Allowance takes a job (or increases their hours) for at least 5 weeks, regardless of income.

To qualify the person must have received Income Support or Jobseeker's Allowance, Incapacity Benefit, Severe Disablement Allowance (or a combination of any) for at least 26 weeks continuously. An extended payment will be paid automatically if the person claiming informs Jobcentre Plus that they have started work or increased their hours within four weeks of so doing (preferably beforehand).

If someone has had a Lone Parent Income Support Run On, they will receive two weeks Extended Housing and Council Tax Benefit afterwards.

Housing Costs Run On

A system which mirrors Extended Housing and Council Tax Benefits for people taking up a job for at least 16 hours a week, (or 24 hours if a partner is taking up work), and the job is expected to last at least five weeks. They must also have had an amount for mortgage interest included in their Income Support or Income-Based Jobseeker's Allowance and have received one of these benefits for at least 26 weeks.

Any mortgage interest paid under a run-on is paid to the person claiming, not their lender.

Housing Costs 52 Week Linking Period

This is for people under 60 who go back onto Income Support or Income-Based Jobseeker's Allowance from full time work or a New Deal or Employment Zone scheme within 52 weeks of leaving these benefits. The normal waiting period before receiving help with mortgage or loan interest is waived (people aged 60 or over do not have a waiting period).

To qualify, people must have been receiving help with their housing costs through Income Support or Income-Based Jobseeker's Allowance before they went into work. Otherwise, there is a twelve week linking period.

Permitted Work

Part-time work allowed for people on Incapacity Benefit.

Linking Periods for Incapacity Benefit

Some people can go off Incapacity Benefit and into work, then back on to the same rate they were receiving before they started work. This linking period can last for up to 52 weeks for some people who move off Incapacity Benefit after at least 196 days incapacity for work and into work or a government training scheme within one week of their Incapacity Benefit ending and Jobcentre Plus are notified about the start of work.

There is also a two year linking rule for certain people who undertake particular training.

In addition, it is established caselaw that a move into work does not give grounds to revise Disability Living or Attendance Allowances, though from time to time one hears of such things happening.

Voluntary Work

See individual benefit entries for information about how people on benefit can undertake voluntary work.

Other help with entry to work or training

A wide range of additional practical help is now available through Jobcentre Plus (for example in Employment Zones or for people with a disability).

Chapter Twenty-four: Other Welfare to Work initiatives

The following part looks at:

- Action Teams
- Ambition
- Employment Zones
- New Deal Young People
- New Deal 25 Plus
- New Deal 50 Plus
- New Deal Lone Parents
- New Deal Partners
- Step Up
- Work Based Learning for Adults
- Work Trials.

This captures in brief some information about other programmes and pilots, whose primary aim is to move participants into sustainable work as quickly as possible, as well as a number of other programmes and services that may be applicable to you.

These programme elements all cite priority and grant early entry for people who have disabilities or learning problems as well as those who have recently left residential care. Your Jobcentre Plus adviser or broker will often be able to refer you to another programme if, after consultation with you, it is found to offer you better prospects for employment and financial gain.

Action Teams for Jobs

Aims

Action Teams (ATs) aim to increase the numbers of people in work in areas that have high unemployment and a lot of people from ethnic minority backgrounds. They focus on the hardest to help and most inactive clients in the local labour market. They aim to secure sustainable employment for clients and it does not matter whether you are claiming benefits or not. ATs are not a programme.

No one is excluded from the help of an AT unless they live outside the area in which the AT operates. Clients are usually asked for their postcode when they first come into contact with an AT for this reason.

ATs operate from outreach sites on local housing estates. There are also 24 mobile units that take the work of the ATs out to those in the community and make links with employers locally.

Action Teams currently operate in 63 areas. These are:

Barnsley & Rotherham
Barrow-in-Furness
Birmingham North
Birmingham South
Blackburn-with-Darwen
Blaenau Gwent
Brent
Brighton & Hove
Caerphilly
Chester-le-Street
Cornwall
Doncaster
Dundee
Easington
East Ayrshire
Glasgow Central
Glasgow North
Glasgow South
Glasgow West
Greenwich
Hackney
Halton
Haringey
Hartlepool
Highlands & Islands
Islington
Kingston upon Hull
Knowsley
Lewisham
Liverpool Central
Liverpool North
Liverpool South
Manchester Central
Manchester North
Manchester South
Merthyr Tydfil
Middlesbrough
Neath Port Talbot
Newcastle-upon-Tyne
Newham
North Lanarkshire
North West Wales
Nottingham
Plymouth
Redcar & Cleveland
Rhondda Cynon Taff
Salford
Sefton
Sheffield
South Tyneside
Southwark
St Helens
Stockton on Tees
Sunderland
Thanet
Tower Hamlets
Waltham Forest
Wansbeck
Wear Valley
West Dunbartonshire
West Wales & The Valleys
Wirral
Wolverhampton

Ambition

Who is Ambition for?

The following eligibility criteria are currently being implemented so may be subject to change:

a) participants on any of the New Deals, including NDDP

b) people who have been unemployed for 52 weeks (or 26 weeks in Manchester and Merseyside) and are in receipt directly or indirectly of one of the following qualifying benefits:

- Incapacity Benefit
- Severe Disablement Allowance
- Jobseeker's Allowance, including those signing for credits only
- Automatic Credits
- Income Support
- Maternity Benefit.

Skills levels vary dependent on the technical content of the job and training. You may therefore be asked to complete assessments of literacy, numeracy and practical skills, along with a structured interview, to determine suitability, which may take place at an open day with the employer present. The programme is voluntary therefore no benefit sanctions are applied if a participant leaves.

Ambition:Construction

The initiative aims to deliver sustainable employment and an NVQ level two or SVQ level three qualification in one of the construction trades: carpenters and joiners; bricklayers; painters and decorators; plasterers, roofers and glaziers. Trainees will achieve appropriate Construction Skills Certification Scheme (CSCS) cards to further enhance their employability.

Ambition:Construction is currently operating in nine locations:

- Nottingham
- Leeds
- Greater Manchester
- Greater Merseyside
- Coventry and Warwickshire
- Paddington (London)
- Aberdeen
- Edinburgh, Lothian and the Borders
- Forth Valley and Dunbartonshire.

Ambition:Energy

Ambition:Energy aims to place 4,500 customers in work over three years in a number of energy sector occupations including: Gas Network Operatives, Domestic Gas Installers, Meter Exchange Operatives, Water Leakage Technician and Engineering Construction trades.

Ambition:Energy differs from the other Ambition initiatives in that it is not limited to a small number of pilot locations. Individual courses are established to meet specific employer recruitment requirements, ensuring the best chance of employment for those successfully completing training. Over 50 courses have been run so far across England, Scotland and Wales.

Ambition:Health

Ambition:Health was launched on 28 April 2004 by Work and Pensions Secretary Andrew Smith. Ambition:Health aims to help unemployed people find work in the National Health Service (NHS).

Jobcentre Plus and the National Employment Panel have developed the programme – like the other Ambitions – but this time the partners in the process have been the NHS and the Learning and Skills Council rather than businesses.

Completed details have not yet emerged but the first Ambition:Health pilots will take place in Merseyside in September 2004 and in South Yorkshire (initially in Barnsley and Rotherham and later expanding to Sheffield and Doncaster) from January 2005.

Ambition:IT

Ambition:IT aims to find people jobs in two areas of work, namely, IT Service Delivery (Systems Support) and Development and Implementation (IT Software Development).

Ambition:IT is being run in three locations:

- Merseyside (the eligibility criteria is six months plus unemployed)
- Greater Manchester (the eligibility criteria is six months plus unemployed)
- Lancashire West (the eligibility criteria is twelve months plus unemployed)
- Leeds
- Birmingham and Solihull
- South Yorkshire.

Ambition:Retail

Ambition:Retail aims to prepare participants for first level retail management in addition to other job opportunities.

Ambition:Retail operates in four locations:

- Cardiff
- Gateshead
- Glasgow
- South Bristol.

Employment Zones

Employment Zones (EZ) were originally designed to help long term unemployed people aged 25 or over find sustainable employment. They operate in 15 areas with high levels of long-term unemployment.

Geographical Coverage

Brent (services provided by Reed in Partnership, Working Links and WorkDirections)

Haringey (services provided by Reed in Partnership, Working Links and WorkDirections)

Brighton and Hove (services provided by Working Links)

Glasgow City (services provided by Reed in Partnership, Working Links and The Wise Group)

Liverpool and Sefton (services provided by Reed in Partnership, Pelcombe Training Ltd and Pertemps Employment Alliance)

Middlesbrough, Redcar and Cleveland (services provided by Pertemps Employment Alliance)

North West Wales (services provided by Working Links)

Tower Hamlets (services provided by Reed in Partnership, Working Links and TNG Workskills)

Newham (services provided by Reed in Partnership, Working Links and TNG Workskills)

Birmingham (services provided by Pertemps Employment Alliance, Working Links and WorkDirections)

Doncaster and Bassetlaw (services provided by Reed in Partnership)

Nottingham City (services provided by WorkDirections)

Plymouth (services provided by Working Links)

Heads of the Valley, Caerphilly and Torfaen (services provided by Working Links)

Southwark (services provided by Reed in Partnership and WorkDirections)

New Deal for Young People

If you are aged between 18 and 24, and have been claiming Jobseeker's Allowance for six months, entry to NDYP is compulsory.

There are three stages to the NDYP:

- **Gateway** - up to four calendar months assessing your needs and developing an individually tailored Action Plan to help you find a job which includes weekly 30 minute interviews with a personal adviser or Job Broker, attending job search and skills courses and access to careers advice and guidance.

- **Four NDYP options** – if you are still unemployed at the end of the Gateway, your personal adviser will arrange a package of full-time help to meet your specific needs, which may include work experience with an employer or voluntary organisation, training for a specific job, courses to develop the skills that employers want and practical help with applying for jobs and interview practice.

- **Follow-through** - If you have completed your option and remain without a job, you will have to re-claim Jobseeker's Allowance. At this point, you will be referred back to your New Deal personal adviser, who will start a follow-through period, in which you will receive intensive help to find jobs, which includes access to specialist programmes and measures where there are complex barriers to work because of disability. The follow–through period can last for up to four months, during which time you will have interviews with your New Deal personal adviser. There is no set frequency for these meetings, as your adviser will agree a course of action that best suits you.

New Deal for 25 Plus

All long-term (18 months or over) Jobseeker's Allowance claimants aged 25–49 years must participate in the New Deal 25 Plus (ND25+).

There are three stages to ND25+:

- **Gateway** – up to four calendar months including weekly meetings with a Jobcentre Plus adviser, where you will receive careers advice, help with communication skills, job searches, interview techniques and confidence building. It may be possible to for an adviser to offer subsidised employment in conjunction with existing Jobcentre Plus programmes, for example Work Trials, Access to work and Subsidised Employment.

- **Mandatory Intensive Activity Period** - If you have not found work by the end of the Gateway, you will move into the Intensive Activity Period (IAP) which aims to address deep-seated barriers to work and consists of flexible packages of support tailored to suit your individual needs. In almost all cases IAP activities will last for a minimum of 30 hours a week, over 5 days for between 13 and 26 weeks, including a training allowance equivalent to your Jobseeker's Allowance plus a top-up, currently £15.38, unless you are on some form of waged provision where you are considered by the Jobcentre Plus personal adviser to be relatively job ready, Work Placements may be made available. Education and training opportunities exist during which you will receive an allowance equivalent to Jobseeker's Allowance but no top-up payment. There is also a self-employment that aims to prepare you for setting up and running a successful business.

- **Follow-through** - If you have been unsuccessful in gaining employment at this stage you will move into follow-through for a period of up to 6 weeks, which consists of additional specialist support. For clients who require additional support the period will be extended up to a maximum of 13 weeks. When you leave the New Deal programme it is hoped that it is because you have secured employment. However it may be that you have to claim another benefit such as Incapacity Benefit, or that you have to return to re-claim Jobseeker's Allowance.

New Deal for 50 Plus

New Deal for 50 Plus offers a route back into paid employment from long-term unemployment (26 weeks or over) for older workers. It is entirely voluntary which means you will not lose any benefits if you decide not to take part.

You are helped to find employment initially through a series of about six thirty-minute interviews with your personal adviser over a period of between three and six months, depending on your needs. If you are disabled, you may be referred to a Disability Employment Adviser if this is believed to be more appropriate than the support provided by a New Deal personal adviser.

The programme looks at skills training opportunities where a training grant of up to £1,500 may be available towards tuition fees. Your New Deal personal adviser may also discuss with you the benefits of doing voluntary work, which you could do to develop and maintain new and existing skills, provide an up to date reference, open up job opportunities or provide you with a talking point at interviews.

Whilst on New Deal 50 Plus, you have access to a range of other schemes, which include:

- Work Based Learning for Adults
- Work Trials
- Travel to Interview Scheme
- Programme Centres.

New Deal for Lone Parents

The New Deal for Lone Parents (NDLP) is designed to help lone parents improve their job readiness and is made up of a series of interviews between you and the New Deal personal adviser. Your Adviser will offer you a package of support including advice on job vacancies, ways in which you can update your skills, self-employment training and by explaining what benefits and incentives are available to help you when you start work such as the Training Premium, Childcare Subsidy and the Adviser Discretion Fund. You will not be compelled to participate in the NDLP programme although you can volunteer to join at any time. You are eligible to participate if you are aged 16 or over, have a dependant child under 16, are not working or working less than 16 hours a week.

If you are a healthcare professional, you could go on the NHS-funded return to practice course.

If you live in London, Birmingham, Leeds/Bradford, Liverpool, Manchester or Glasgow you may be eligible for an enhanced package of NDLP support.

New Deal for Partners

The New Deal for Partners (NDP) is a voluntary employment programme, which gives partners of benefit claimants access to a personal adviser who can provide an individually tailored package of help and support. It is designed to help partners improve their job readiness and increase their employment opportunities. You will not be compelled to participate in the NDP programme although you can volunteer to join at any time. A personal adviser will be able to offer you advice and information about jobs, Jobcentre Plus programmes, training, Adviser's Discretion Fund, Training Premium, self-employment, availability of affordable local childcare, and substitute care for carers.

Your partner must be claiming one of the following benefits:

- Incapacity Benefit
- Severe Disablement Allowance
- Carer's Allowance
- Jobseeker's Allowance
- Income Support
- From 25 October 2004, Working Tax Credit.

You must be married to or living with the main claimant.

Can I join NDP? Answer the following questions to find out		
Benefits Is your partner claiming Jobseeker's Allowance, Income Support, Incapacity Benefit, Carer's Allowance or Severe Disablement Allowance, Working Tax Credit (from October 2004)?	YES	NO
Work Are you not working, or working less than 24 hours a week on average (16 hours a week for partners claiming Working Tax Credit)?	YES	NO
Benefits Are you NOT making a Joint Claim for Jobseeker's Allowance?	YES	NO
If you answered YES to every question, then you probably can join NDP If you answered NO to any of the questions, then you probably cannot join NDP		

StepUP

Aim

StepUP is specifically aimed at claimants who have been through the New Deal at least once and are still claiming Jobseeker's Allowance.

StepUP aims to increase your work experience via employment lasting up to 50 weeks paying at least a minimum wage, and in this way provides you with a reference that will help you get another job, as well as giving you the satisfaction of working in a real job as opposed to being on a scheme.

To be eligible you must:

- have claimed Jobseeker's Allowance for at least 18 months
- have taken part in either NDYP or ND25+
- have continued to claim Jobseeker's Allowance at the end of New Deal.

You may be exempt from taking part in StepUP if you are found not to be better off financially in a StepUP job offered to you.

Additionally, you will be given the opportunity to participate in WORKSTEP over StepUP if you are found to fulfill the eligibility criteria for both StepUP and WORKSTEP, and if it is assessed that WORKSTEP is the best option and supports your specific disability.

Under these circumstances you will be exempt from StepUP. However, if exemption from StepUP is given you cannot then opt out of WORKSTEP, and if StepUP is the best option for you, you will be referred to StepUP in the same way as a non-disabled customer.

It is currently operating in 20 areas:

- Leeds
- Bristol
- Sunderland
- Sandwell
- Knowlsey
- Cardiff
- Sheffield
- Rotherham
- Hackney
- Bradford
- Wrexham
- Coventry
- Lambeth
- Great Yarmouth
- East Ayrshire
- Manchester
- Burnley
- Oldham
- Dundee
- Greenwich.

Work Based Learning for Adults

Jobcentre Plus is responsible for Work Based Learning for Adults (WBLA) in England, however, in Wales, the National Assembly for Wales delivers WBLA. The Enterprise Networks administers Training for Work (TFW) in Scotland.

The aim of WBLA is to:

- give you the skills to improve your employability
- help you build your confidence and develop those skills you lack
- meet the skill needs of local employers.

WBLA comprises: Basic Employability Training; Short Job Focused Training; Longer Occupational Training and; Self-Employment Provision.

Eligibility

WBLA is an adult training programme and is usually only available if you:

- are aged 25 or over; there is no upper age limit
- have been registered as unemployed for six months or more (12 months or more of Longer Occupational Training)
- are in receipt of a qualifying benefit (including Jobseeker's Allowance, NI credits, Incapacity Benefit, Severe Disablement Allowance, Income Support and Maternity Benefit).

Early Entry Eligibility

If you are aged 25 or over, you may be eligible for early entry to WBLA regardless of your length of unemployment, for example, if you are a refugee who has been given permission to remain in the UK and claim Jobseeker's Allowance, if you have a disability or if you need help with your spoken English.

The broad range of eligibility combined with the fact that you can refer yourself means that as a newcomer you can join if you are also from abroad even if you are classed as a Person Subject to Immigration Control (PSIC) (and so normally excluded from being able to receive benefits) or you have other restrictions on your benefit entitlement.

WBLA provision is delivered through the following four programmes:

Basic Employability Training (BET)

BET is particularly focused on helping those who need assistance in overcoming severe basic skills needs and English for Speakers of Other Languages (ESOL) difficulties. The Basic Skills Standards have three Levels: Entry Level, Level 1 and Level 2. BET helps you to improve your basic skills of literacy and numeracy by helping you to reach a standard at least to Basic Skills Standard at Level 1, or as a minimum to Entry Level. Prior to BET, you will need to attend an Initial Assessment to identify your level of basic skills.

Short Job Focused Training (SJFT)

The overall aim is to help you gain soft and occupational skills to enable you to get a job. SJFT also includes Work Placements. SJFT lasts for a maximum of six weeks and you must complete a minimum of 16 hours of activity each week, over five days. SJFT provision is practical and hands-on, designed to impart straightforward, well defined skills whilst meeting the needs of the labour market and being tailored to your individual needs.

Longer Occupational Training (LOT)

The overall aim of LOT provision is to help you acquire new skills or update existing ones through tailored work-focused training to help you find work. LOT lasts for a minimum of 7 weeks and up to a maximum of 52 weeks. You must complete a minimum of 16 hours of activity each week, over five days. LOT seeks to bring together employers and providers to provide work-focused training modules designed to deliver specific soft and occupational skills to prepare you for work. LOT helps you reach local recruitment standards, based on agreements brokered with employers with skill shortages or recruitment shortfalls, or to meet the needs of new employers moving into the district.

Self-Employment Provision (SEP)

This offers you the opportunity to move into unsupported self-employment. SEP also offers support to those participants who decide during their time on the provision, that they would rather seek employment with an employer than be self-employed. SEP provides you with access to good quality advice and support and, also, where appropriate, the opportunity to undertake a period of test trading. This allows you to experience the realities of self-employment while continuing to receive help and support from the training provider. SEP has three distinct stages: Stage 1 (one day), Stage 2 (part-time over four weeks), and Stage 3 (maximum period of 26 weeks).

Getting onto Work Based Learning for Adults

There are several ways of getting onto WBLA, for example you could:

- be referred by your personal adviser at Jobcentre Plus
- be recruited directly by a local training provider
- apply by yourself because you heard about a particular programme that you believe would meet your needs
- you are also likely to be referred by your Jobcentre Plus personal adviser at the six month Restart interview.

Recruited by a training provider

Local training providers can recruit people onto their programmes. For example, you may see adverts in your local paper about programmes and courses designed to help you improve your employability.

The decision on whether you take part in WBLA provision does, however, rest with your Jobcentre Plus adviser.

Refer yourself

You could ask to be put on a WBLA programme. For example:

- you may know what programme you want to do in order to make yourself more employable

- you may have heard about a relevant programme from a friend or relative, or
- you could take the initiative and ask about local programmes which you think will help you.

Work Trials

Work Trials are entirely voluntary and last for a period of up to 15 working days, giving employers the chance to try someone out for a particular job before deciding whether to employ them. It provides the opportunity for employers to consider long-term unemployed people by enabling employers to see whether they are suitable for the work.

The key benefits are:

- you can decide whether the job is suitable without losing your benefit: if you leave a Work Trial or decide you do not want the job your benefit is not affected
- you will be paid meals and travel expenses
- it gives you the opportunity to prove you can do the job
- it is a good way to persuade an employer to try you out
- it is an opportunity to find out what problems you may have in a working environment and get support to overcome them.

A Work Trial can be arranged by a Jobcentre Plus personal adviser or you can suggest a Work Trial to a potential employer. The employer should contact Jobcentre Plus before you begin the trial.

Eligibility

If you are a person with disabilities and unemployed you can participate regardless of your age or how long you have been unemployed.

> However, if you are claiming Incapacity Benefit or Severe Disablement Allowance, then you must be advised that participation on a Work Trial may affect your entitlement to benefits.

The working hours of the Work Trial should reflect the normal contracted hours of the job, not including overtime. They should not be over 40 hours a week, except where the standard working week is over 40 hours. In this case, the personal adviser must ensure that there is a genuine vacancy and that you are aware of and agree with the working hours. When you are participating in a Work Trial, you will continue to receive your full benefit, and can claim for travel expenses up to £10 a day and meal expenses up to £3.00 a day.

You may be offered the job after the Work Trial and accept it, If however you decide not to take it, your benefit entitlement will not be affected. In this situation, your Jobcentre Plus personal adviser will agree a further course of action with you.

Part Three: In learning and the workplace

Chapter Twenty-five: An overview of the Disability Discrimination Act 1995 (DDA) and the definition of disability

Kath Hoskisson

The DDA was passed in 1995 to introduce new measures aimed at ending the discrimination which many disabled people faced when trying to get or stay in work, accessing education, or being able to participate in everyday activities such as shopping and receiving services.

It is split into four parts, which were introduced in stages to allow companies to adjust to the new legislation and prepare action plans for reapplying the law:

Part One deals with the Definition of disability (see p227)

Part Two Looks at Employment provisions (see Chapters 26-29) and duties of trade organisations (see Chapter 30) to their disabled members and applicants

Part Three addresses access to goods, facilities, services and premises and is split into three sections:

3.1 ensures that people with disabilities are not treated less favourably than others, (see Chapter 31).

3.2 Service Providers have to make reasonable alterations to how they deliver services, (see Chapter 32).

3.3 Service Providers have to make permanent physical adjustments to their premises, (see Chapter 33).

Part Four focuses on the Education part of the Act (see Chapter 34). It is also known as the Special Educational Needs and Disability Act 2001 or SENDA.

It stipulates that Education Establishments can no longer discriminate against a disabled learner for a reason related to their disability. They must already make practical alterations in the way that they provide the teaching, which came into force in September 2003, and in some cases they will have to alter the actual structure of the buildings where classes are held, which comes into force in September 2005.

This separate part for education was required to allow colleges and universities enough time to come into line with the rest of the organisations in the country who already come under Parts 1–3.

There has also been an amendment to the law by the Disability Discrimination Act 1995 (Amendment) Regulations 2003, which comes into force at the same time as Part 3.3. These Regulations have been incorporated into the legislation described in the following sections.

Some of the Act is already in force, and some areas are coming into force later this year.

Part 1,2 and 3.1, came into force in October 1996
Part 3.2 became enforceable in October 1999
Part 4 came into force in September 2002
Part 3.3 comes into force in October 2004

In addition to the Act there were also provisions made to form a Disability Rights Commission to oversee the implementation of the Act and provide support for people with disabilities.

The DDA 1995 makes it illegal to discriminate against people with disabilities by:

- treating a disabled person less favourably for a reason relating to their disability
- failing to make reasonable adjustments to avoid placing a disabled person at a substantial disadvantage in comparison with someone who is not disabled.

It protects disabled people from discrimination, victimisation and harassment.

If you are disabled, or have had a disability in the past, the Disability Discrimination Act 1995 (DDA) makes it against the law for you to be discriminated against in employment and access to Goods Facilities and Service.

There is one other part that is worth summarising, but doesn't really apply unless you are looking at self-employment or setting up your own business, and that is the management, buying or renting of land or property.

The law says that a landlord cannot refuse to sign an agreement with a person with a disability unless there is a good reason not to do so. They must not presume that just because a person has a disability they are unable to understand the nature of the agreement they are going to sign.

However, when the property or land has been rented the landlord does not have to make physical alterations to those premises, unless they are specifically requested to do so. What they must do is give permission for the leaseholder to make these alterations themselves if they want to for the duration of their lease. This is not the case for areas or land that the landlord allows members of the public to use. In these circumstances the landlord is the service provider and must make alterations under Part 3 of the Act.

If tenants are providing services to the general public from rented accommodation, they will have a duty under Part 3 of the

Act to make sure that their services are accessible to people with disabilities. Where public areas make it difficult for the public and disabled people to use the services provided by that tenant, the leasor can ask the Landlord to change them. If this difficulty continues, the Service Provider will have to look at other ways of providing a service as detailed in the Access to goods and services section.

It is worth remembering though that if permission is given to a service provider or employer, the landlord is within their right to ask for the building to be put back to its original state at the end of the lease. However, if this alteration is to the benefit of the landlord by making the building more accessible, then they should consider leaving it as it is.

The landlord also has to change their rules and actions to ensure that they do not discriminate against a disabled person, and provide supplementary aids or services that make it easier for a disabled person to let the premises.

This could be changing a policy to allow assistant dogs to be on the premises, or reading the lease agreement to a visually impaired person.

What they don't have to do is provide an extra aid that is required permanently for a disabled person. For example they don't have to provide a wheelchair for someone with mobility problems who normally uses a wheelchair in their everyday activities.

Finally one phrase that comes up repeatedly in the Act relates to Reasonable Adjustments.

This means in every case that the person involved (employer, service provider etc) has to come up with alternative ways of doing things that ensures that a person with a disability can participate in the same way as everyone else. It also relates to changing the structure of buildings, both inside and out, so that everyone can use them. Examples of reasonable adjustments will be demonstrated in this chapter as much as possible, but you must remember that everyone is different and what makes things accessible for one person may not make it accessible for everyone.

Most employers and service providers are willing to listen to what people with disabilities have to say about getting to use their services or being able to be a good employee. So as long as they think that they are doing something worthwhile and won't get into trouble for it, most people will change to meet your requirements.

In the case of employment there are very few occasions when things cannot be changed to accommodate a disabled person's needs, as long as it doesn't mean a substantial upheaval for the company or they are physically unable to do so because of building regulations or restricted space.

Service providers can be more difficult to persuade, as it often means a large initial outlay for which they cannot see any return. However, small changes in stores on how they provide certain services can overcome these with no extra cost.

There are rules that govern what service providers have to do and in what circumstances they do not, which is covered in more detail in the Access to goods and services section.

Part 1 - The Definition of Disability

For the first time in history the law defines disability and a person with disabilities from a social perspective rather than a medical angle. This fairly wider definition is still the subject of debate and has been amended from the original one through the Amendment Regulations 2003.

Much of the definition is being further clarified through the courts, where people have taken their employer or the service provider to Court for reasons relating to their disability and discrimination against them which has broken the DDA law. The

Court then decides if a person has a disability in relation to the Act before proceeding. It is usually up to the person with the disability to prove they have a disability as described in the DDA's definition.

The DDA describes a disabled person as 'anyone with a physical or mental impairment, which has a substantial and long-term adverse effect upon their ability to carry out normal day-to-day activities'.

This also counts as a definition when people have had a disability as described by the Act, but have since recovered or the condition is in remission, as long as when they did have it, and it met all the criteria such as being long-term and having an adverse effect of their normal day to day activities.

In order to understand fully what the definition means, it needs to be broken down into its component parts. Only then can a person look at it clearly to decide whether or not they are classed as having a disability within the meaning of the Act.

Physical impairment includes a weakening or change of a part of the body caused through illness, by accident, or from birth, such as blindness, deafness, heart disease, the paralysis of a limb or severe disfigurement and many other different predicaments.

Mental Impairment includes Learning Difficulties and all recognized Mental Illnesses such as those specifically mentioned in the World Health Organisation's International Classification of Diseases.

Substantial - This is open to personal interpretation as the guidance to this section of the law says that it doesn't have to be severe, but needs to be more than minor or trivial. However, severe to one person may not be severe to another, and the courts have not yet agreed to a set standard. The disabled person has to prove that it is substantial to them.

Long-Term adverse effect means that the disability has lasted or is likely to last more than 12 months. This effectively rules out conditions such as broken limbs which are not related to a serious medical condition.

Normal Day-to-Day Activities. The law states that the disability must have an effect on a person's ability to carry out one or more of the following activities:

- a person's mobility
- manual dexterity
- physical co-ordination
- continence
- ability to lift, carry or move everyday objects
- speech
- hearing
- eyesight
- memory
- ability to concentrate
- ability to learn or understand
- ability to identify risks and physical dangers.

What it doesn't include is the ability to work, because no particular form of work is normal for most people.

The important rule

The most important thing to remember when looking at the effects of a disability against the definition above is to only focus on the disability itself without any medical treatment or equipment. For example diabetes without being controlled with insulin, or hearing without a hearing aid, or the pain one could be in without pain relief.

The only exception to this rule is where poor eyesight is improved by wearing glasses or contact lenses. In this case the effects that count are only those which remain even with the glasses or lenses.

The new DDA 1995 (Amendment) Regulations 2003 now bring people who have (or have had) Cancer, HIV or Multiple Sclerosis into the definition as recognised conditions.

The conditions that don't count as a disability

There are certain specific conditions that don't count as a disability under the above definition despite the fact that they meet the various requirements such as long term, substantial and having a detrimental effect on the normal day-to-day activities.

These are:

- tattoos and non-medical piercings which are lifestyle choices
- a tendency to steal, set fires, or physically or sexually abuse others
- exhibitionism and voyeurism
- hayfever, where it doesn't aggravate the effects of any other existing condition.
- addiction or dependency on alcohol, nicotine or any other substance other than that being medically prescribed. (This includes heroin substitutes which can be prescribed but don't count).

Chapter Twenty-six: Employment provisions

Historically there was a law which stated that large organisations had to have three percent of their workforce who had a disability. This proved very unhelpful for disabled people who often felt as though they were there because of their disability rather than their abilities.

The Disability Discrimination Act 1995 looked to address this and ensure that people with disabilities were able to compete for jobs on the open market and on an equal footing with non-disabled people. So the old quota system was removed and the following rules put into place to assist this process.

Originally in the DDA, employers who had less than 15 employees were exempt from the employment requirements of the Act, but with the advent of the Amendment Regulations 2003 this is changing and from October 2004 all employers will have to follow the duties.

The Act says that there are two ways that employers can unlawfully discriminate against an employee or job applicant with a disability. These are:

- by treating them less favourably than other people because of their disability or without a good reason
- by not making reasonable adjustments because of their disability, once again without justification or good reason.

> The one most important thing to remember when looking at employment is that unless you tell your employer or potential employer that you have a disability, they will not be able to assist you with any adjustments that need to be made.

Exemption from the DDA with regard to employment

There are still certain types of employment which are not covered by the law, and their employers therefore do not have any duties to follow towards people with disabilities.

These are:

- employees who work wholly or largely outside of Great Britain
- members of the Armed Forces
- employees who work onboard ships, aircraft or hovercraft.

Police officers, fire fighters, barristers, Prison Officers and partners in business partnerships will be covered by the Act from October 2004 because of the Amendment Regulations 2003. In the past these were also exempt.

Chapter Twenty-seven: The business case for employing disabled people

Sometimes employers feel very anxious about employing someone with a disability. This can be because they do not understand about disability or they fear the supposed extra costs involved of employing someone with a disability. But in either case the fears can be removed through discussing the positive reasons for employing someone with a disability and showing how this can actually benefit their company.

Most people who have a disability can work alongside non-disabled employees without any, or with very little, extra help. Others may need some changes to the working surroundings or in the companies working practices, but these alterations can be straightforward and cheap to put into practice.

Research has shown that there are benefits to companies in having a wide and varied range of employees, especially those who have disabilities.

These include:

- having more choice over who they can employ
- employers have found that people with disabilities tend to stay in their jobs for longer and have a strong loyalty to their work as well as good punctuality and low absentee (sickness) rates. People with disabilities tend not to have time off sick unless it directly relates to their disability, and if they are looking for work, their disability is nearly always already controlled
- keeping someone at work who develops a disability whilst they still work for the employer generally costs less than having to recruit and training someone new

- employing someone with a disability can help to increase the number of people using a service provided by that organisation and research has shown that up to £50 billion of customer money is available to the market as a result of spending by people with disabilities, their families and friends

- employing someone with a disability can also boost staff morale as they can see that the organisation is looking to be more varied and representative of the local society in their personnel

- the benefits that a person with disabilities can bring through the changes in the organisation that occur can often help other employees and customers.

Employers always want the right person for the job and the Disability Discrimination Act 1995 can assist them to do this. By helping employers to comply with the DDA and the Amendment Regulations, a person with a disability can help the employer promote good working relationships with their employees, by demonstrating that they offer employment on an equal footing as everyone else, regardless of the person's disability.

If an employer does not follow the requirements of the Act or Amendment regulations, they risk costly court proceedings, bad publicity and could even end up at an Employment Tribunal.

Chapter Twenty-eight: An employer's duties and alterations that could be considered

Within the employment field a person with a disability is protected by the law if they are:

- job applicants
- self-employed
- employees
- contractors or
- on work placement (volunteers).

Moreover, they are protected during all stages of recruitment and employment:

- in the adverts
- in the job specification
- in the way application forms are written and how people are expected to fill them in
- in the interview – including the time and place of interview as well as during the interview
- in any assessment technique
- in the terms on which any job offer is made
- in the terms and conditions of service
- in induction arrangements
- in any opportunities for promotion, training, or transfer / secondment opportunity, including refusal of these
- in any opportunities to receive employee benefits and refusing these
- in occupational pension schemes
- in the case of redundancy or dismissal.

What this means is that a person with a disability is given the opportunity to work on an equal footing with everyone else and is chosen on merit rather than against the old quota system.

Often companies advertise with the two tick symbol on their advert and all their literature. This symbol is called the 'positive about disabled people' symbol and is given to employing bodies by Jobcentre Plus when they put into practice five different actions relating to the way that the organisation and their employees work. Organisations carrying this symbol are checked every year to make sure they are still following the rules and not discriminating against people with disabilities.

Job specifications or job descriptions now only have the essential items on it that are required for the job.

> For example, 'Car Driver' is not now considered to be appropriate on a job specification unless the job actually requires the person to drive i.e. lorry driver, bus driver, or community transport driver. The public transport system and the Government's policy of encouraging people to stay off the roads, has rendered this an unworthy criteria to put on job descriptions.

Any person with a disability who meets the job specification should automatically get an interview for the job, especially if the company uses the two tick symbol.

Some jobs require application forms and some only ask for Curriculum Vitae, which is a list of your qualifications, skills and work history. The Disability Employment Advisor (DEA) at your local Jobcentre Plus can provide help with these (see page 163).

For those people who have language difficulties it is important that you liaise with your DEA who will assist you with completing any forms, or ensure that you can provide a spoken version if required.

Often companies required their potential employees to take assessment tests prior to interview to see if that person is capable for the job.

Examples of Assessment types can include:

- psychometric testing
- report writing
- shorthand
- typing or word processing skills
- specific job related tasks.

In all assessment tests, the employer has to give due attention to any special requirements a person with a disability has. This can include extra time; specialist equipment; or support. In some cases tests are not appropriate at all and the Disability Employment Advisor at your local Jobcentre Plus can help you and advise the employer if required.

Before the interview takes place, employers are supposed to ask if there are any special requirements that would benefit you, or that they need to take into consideration before the day.

These could include:

- an accessible building – ramps, lifts, on the ground floor, accessible toilets, and so on
- braille literature
- an interview at a particular time – in the morning or in the afternoon
- a British Sign Language interpreter
- a loop system
- someone to guide a visually impaired person around the building
- an advocate during the interview process for people with learning difficulties.

During the interview employers should focus on your abilities rather than your disabilities. Many companies are aware of the Access to Work Scheme, which is Government Funded through Jobcentre Plus, which will assist with many aspects of enabling a person with a disability to do the job they are applying for. If you are asked about your disabilities, describe how you would be able to do the job in question with or without alterations either to the duties involved or in the fabric of the building. If you think alterations may need to be made, make it clear that funding will be able to be provided from the Access to Work Scheme. Always ensure that you are positive about the things you can bring to the company rather than focusing of what they may see as negative aspects. The interview is a chance to sell yourself and the DDA 1995 now ensures that you have that opportunity.

What employers have to do

Most employers want to help employees or job applicants who have disabilities, and are willing to make adjustments, but they aren't always sure what is required or how to go about it.

A general starting point for any employer is to consider where their employment arrangements or any physical feature of the workplace are putting people with disabilities at a substantial disadvantage against people without disabilities, and then make changes to resolve these problems. Many alterations can be straightforward and are often inexpensive to do, but the advantages resulting from doing them help other employees or customers.

> One thing to remember about the law in this situation though is that employers do not have to make alterations in anticipation of employing a person with a disability.

An employer is not required to have a disability audit done or put into place any changes just in case a person with a disability applies for a job. Those duties only arise if the employer receives an application for a job from a person with disability or have an employee with a disability, and then it's very much tailored to that individual.

Given that disability has a wide and varied definition, it can be difficult to know when it is reasonable for an employer to make changes in relation to the law. Each case will be individual and unique to the person for whom the changes are being made, so it is always best if the employer talks to the person with a disability to discuss what might be needed. Most of the time these alterations will be cheap, quick and easy to do without much disruption to the workplace, and if more complex changes are needed then the Access to Work Scheme may be able to help.

At present there is no upper limit on cost that might be considered an unreasonable amount to pay for an alteration, but where only employment is concerned, Access to Work funding may be applicable.

The types of things that an employer has to take into consideration when looking at changes could be:

- the effectiveness of that change: if a change looks as though it would make no difference to the job applicant or employee and there is evidence to back this up, then an employer is entitled to refuse to do it
- whether it is practical to take a specific action
- whether the costs of doing it, and the amount of disruption it will cause when doing it, has a major financial impact on the business. For instance if job cuts would have to be made as a result of doing it, or the business loses money because production and work has to stop whilst the change is being made
- whether the company can afford it, through finance or other types of resources.

An employer should always make changes when they become aware of a person disability. This could be at the recruitment stage, or after they are employed.

The changes involved might include the arrangements for an interview, how the person is inducted into the company, their terms and conditions of employment, how they are promoted, transferred to another job, trained, or receive benefits that all other employees receive, or in some circumstances dismissed or made redundant.

If an employer is in doubt about what they should do if an employee becomes disabled whilst employed at the company or they receive an application from a person with a disability, then they should contact their local Jobcentre Plus to speak to an advisor. These advisors can offer advice, but not legal advice, and give practical assistance about employing a person with a disability.

Alterations that could be considered are:

Making changes to the premises

Such as ensuring corridors and walkways are free from clutter; brailling names and signs on doors; providing a carpark space near a staff entrance; changing door handles so that they are easier to open; lowering security devices on doors or light switches; lowering shelves or moving regularly used resources to lower shelves; providing Evac chairs to get someone out of a building in the case of a fire. More examples are listed in the access to buildings and facilities section.

Transferring an employee to another job – this is applicable for employees who develop a disability whilst still in employment

For example, changing a job from one that entails lifting and carrying to a desk job if a person has developed mobility problems.

Giving minor duties to another employee, or swapping duties from one person to another

For example if two people are receptionists but also have to do the photocopying for people, which is difficult for the person with a disability to do, and opening the mail which is easier to do, then the other work colleague could do the photocopying in return for the person with a disability opening the mail.

Being flexible about working hours

This can be done for an employee with a disability who may have difficulty at certain times of the day because of medication or other problems; to fit around the availability of a carer; or other reasons.

Allowing time off for rehabilitation, assessment, hospital appointments, or time for treatment relating to their disability

Hospital appointments are difficult to arrange outside of a person's normal working day and a person with a disability is unlikely to take other time off. So allowing them to attend appointments usually means that they will be very committed to that particular employer.

Moving a person's workplace

For instance allowing a person to work on the ground floor if the organisation does not have the equipment to get them to another floor; moving their desk from a difficult to reach place to a more accessible one in the office; ensuring that meetings take place somewhere accessible for the person in question; or other changes discussed with the individual.

Providing training appropriate to their needs

For example send someone on training to learn how to use his or her new specialist equipment, or having someone in to train him or her in the workplace.

Providing specialist equipment, or modifying existing equipment to meet their needs

For instance a text phone (minicom), speech to text software, magnifiers, a fully adjustable chair, and other items as accessed by the person themselves or via Access to Work.

Changing Policies and Procedures

Sometimes just changing the way staff and the company do things can be more helpful than any equipment, training or changes in job.

A policy enabling someone with an assistance dog to work on the premises could help, or training some staff in basic sign language to allow communication with a deaf person in the absence of an interpreter could help.

Sending all staff on Disability Awareness Training is always beneficial to an organisation and there are now national workplace training systems in place to provide this training at people's desks without disrupting work. Setting up a mentoring scheme or support group for people with disabilities can help, as can ensuring that any changes in policies are discussed with employees with disabilities before they take place.

Providing information in a format that employees with disabilities can understand and read, such as large print (always ask what size is appropriate), using different coloured paper for people with dyslexia, or Braille, are all ways of ensuring that everyone receives the same information in the organisation.

These are all ways of ensuring that employees are treated equally in an organisation. But the best way of knowing that the changes are the best for the individual in question is by asking them what changes would help them do their job, and getting an Access to Work assessment done.

Other suggested changes that can be made are, are listed in more detail in the following Access to Work Section.

Chapter Twenty-nine: Access to Work Scheme

The Access to Work Programme is run by Jobcentre Plus, and provides financial assistance towards the extra costs of employing someone with a disability. It is available to anyone who is unemployed, employed or self-employed.

The types of support available:

- a British Sign Language Interpreter or other Deaf or Hearing Impaired Language Interpreter
- a reader at work to assist someone who is blind or has a visual impairment
- a support worker to assist someone with practical help because of their disability, either at work or getting to work
- help towards taxi fares or other transport costs, if they cannot use public transport to get to work because of their disability
- adaptations to a vehicle to enable someone to get to and from work
- specialist equipment or alterations to existing equipment, which is necessary because of an individual's disability. For example: installation of specialist speech or talking software on an existing computer; a touch screen monitor; scanner or electronic reader
- alterations to premises or a working environment necessary because of a person's disability. However, alterations will not be made if they would already be required through part 3.3 of the DDA.

Funding Available

The money available through Access to Work depends upon the employment status of the person with a disability at the time of application.

Unemployed people who are starting a job will get 100% of all the approved costs paid for from Access to Work.

People changing their jobs within a company and thus having new job descriptions will also receive 100% of all the approved costs, as will people starting a new job with a new company.

People who have been employed in the same job by the same organisation for more that six weeks cannot claim costs of anything that falls below £300. However they will be entitled to claim for 80% of all costs after the first £300 up to £10,000 and Access to Work will pay 100% of all costs above £10,000.

For example:

1. A computer plus software, desk, and specialist chair totals £5260

   The company pays for the first £300

   The company then pays 20% of £4960 left = £992

   Leaving a claim from Access to Work of £3968

2. An accessible toilet is required in the workplace costing £22,000

   Access to Work will pay 100% of these costs.

Self-employed people who have been self-employed for six weeks or longer cannot make a claim for anything less than £100, as they are expected to pay this themselves. After this amount Access to Work will pay 90% of the costs up to £10,000 and 100% of the costs above this.

For Example:

1. A self-employed person is assessed as requiring a speech to text computer programme costing £97. The person with a disability is expected to meet this cost through their business.
2. A self-employed person is assessed as requiring a specialist chair which costs £2600. The person with a disability will have to pay the first £100 and then 90% of the total cost = £350. Access to Work will pay the other £2250.

Access to work will pay 100% of approved costs towards travel to work regardless of the person's employment status.

The programme will also pay for 100% of the approved costs of a communicator/interpreter at interview, irrespective of the person's employment status.

If a support for work is assessed to be required for a person with disabilities, Access to Work will pay for 100% of the costs that they have approved towards this support, regardless of the person's employment status.

Applications for Access to Work assistance must be made by the person with a disability rather than the employer and there is a form to complete which is available from a Disability Employment Adviser or any Jobcentre Plus office. Access to Work is managed in different regions across the country and some areas have a helpline rather than workers in Jobcentre Plus. Jobcentre Plus will be able to advise you if this is the case.

Sometimes, the answers and solutions provided by Access to Work may be of benefit to other members of the company, where they can make use of the equipment for themselves as well as the person with a disability. In these instances, Access to Work will estimate the costs incurred by the other staff member's use of the items, and class this as a business benefit, which will be deducted from the cost of the item before it is paid. Access to Work will then pay the proportionate costs, as outlined above, of the rest of the money being claimed.

Access to Work is administered by Jobcentre Plus, and to find out more about the Programme and how to apply in your area, the employee must contact their employment advisor.

Chapter Thirty: Duties of trade unions

Trade unions are often both service providers and employers, and as such will have duties under other areas (Part 2 and Part 3) of the Disability Discrimination Act 1995. They may often use their skills and experience of dealing with service users and employees with disabilities in meeting their clients needs if they have disabilities, and following their specific duties outlined in the Act.

They are also held responsible for making changes even if the only people to know about a disability is a member of staff. They are not allowed to pass this information on because of confidentiality issues.

Therefore the best way of moving forward for trade unions is to make the changes anyway in anticipation of having disabled members or requests for membership from people with disabilities.

Broadly speaking trade unions have to:

- write a policy regarding how staff deal with people with disabilities, and make sure that all their staff and members, whether paid or unpaid, know what it says, how the law works, and how to make reasonable changes to the way in which they work

- tell all their members and staff that discrimination or victimisation as detailed in the DDA will not be tolerated and actually do something about it if someone breaks the rules

- monitor their policies regarding people with disabilities and make sure they are working

- provide disability awareness training for all staff who deal with the general public

- discipline staff who break the rules regarding the treatment of people with disabilities
- write a complaints procedure which can be used by everyone with a disability
- know exactly how to deal with someone who victimises or harasses someone with a disability
- actually talk to people with disabilities about their experiences
- review their membership services and benefits to make sure that someone with a disability can use them.

As with the rules for private clubs, trade unions are not allowed to discriminate against people with disabilities:

- in the way they are offered membership
- by refusing an application for membership
- in any benefits offered to all their members
- by withdrawing membership without good reason
- by changing the terms of membership for the person with a disability but not anyone else.

Trade unions also have to make reasonable changes to their premises if it places that person with a disability at a disadvantage to everyone else.

Chapter Thirty-one: Access to goods and services

The Disability Discrimination Act 1995 makes it unlawful for providers of goods and service to discriminate against members of the public who have disabilities and has been in force since December 1996.

The DDA 1995 and Amendment Regulations 2003, makes discrimination by service and goods providers unlawful if:

- they refuse a service to a person with a disability without good reason. (A service provider can refuse to serve a disabled customer as long as they are able to justify such action, and their reasons have nothing to do with the customer's disability and they would refuse to serve other customers in the same circumstances)
- they provide a service, which is of a lesser standard to a person with a disability without a good reason
- they provide a service on worse terms to a person with a disability
- they fail to make alterations and changes to the way a service is provided so that a person with a disability can use it.

Also from October 2004, the Physical Access (part 3.3) comes into force, which means that service providers need to make alterations and changes to the physical material of their buildings, so that people with disabilities can use them and get to use the services provided in them. This is discussed in more detail in the next section.

Who is covered under the Act?

Anyone who provides goods or a service is covered by these rules, and it doesn't matter how large or small they are, or whether the goods and services are free or not.

They are also responsible for the actions of their employees in relation to providing the services or goods.

There are some exceptions but the following are examples of all those which have to abide by the law:

- hotels
- libraries
- guest houses (bed & breakfast)
- pubs and nightclubs
- shops
- cafes and restaurants
- hairdressers and beauty salons
- estate agents
- banks and building societies
- Housing Associations
- councils including the services provided and the buildings they are provided in
- training providers other than schools, colleges and universities

- mail order, internet and telephone shopping companies
- courts
- solicitors
- doctors, hospitals and clinics
- dentists, chiropodists, and alternative/complementary therapists
- physiotherapists
- investment companies
- churches, temples and other places of worship
- sports centres and other leisure providers
- bus stations, railway stations and airport terminals
- parks
- historic buildings
- museums
- cinemas and theatres
- schools where other activities other than education are offered (i.e. a hall which is used as a polling station, or for a parents evening)
- community centres
- garages and service stations.

Those services that are exempt are:

- education establishments such as schools, colleges and universities (except where they have proven services that are not education related).

The only thing that the DDA requires education establishments to do is publish their information about the organisation and how to get into their school, college or university in an accessible format for people with disabilities. This is usually done at the request of a person with a disability, so that the format is individually tailored to their needs.

However the DDA was supplemented in October 2002 with Special Educational Needs and Disabilities Act 2001 (SENDA), which now make it unlawful for schools, further education colleges and universities to discriminate against students with disabilities. (See chapter 34.)

- transport, such as taxis, buses, coaches, trams, trains, ships, hovercraft, and planes.

The Government has produced guidance on the future production of new trains, which include access for people with disabilities, and new taxis, but this will not come into force for many years. Bus companies are already taking the DDA on board when looking at future production of buses, even though they are not yet legally required to do so. In many parts of the country, trials of new 'kneeling buses' are being held, which are single-deck buses which lower to the kerb at stops so that people with mobility problems and parents with pushchairs can get on. They are also automating bus stops with talking and speaking announcements regarding bus times and numbers, and using tactile paving to demonstrate where bus stops are.

The new Amendment Regulations 2003 will allow the government to introduce more legislation about making other transport accessible to people with disabilities in the future.

> Since April 2001 it has been unlawful in England and Wales for taxi drivers to refuse to carry assistance dogs who are accompanying their disabled owners, and they have to be allowed to remain with them (i.e. not put in the boot of the vehicle). They are also not allowed to charge extra money for this service.
>
> Any driver who refuses to allow this to happen may be found guilty of a criminal offence and fined, unless they have a very good reason for denying the dog access, which is usually medical and requires evidence of that from their Doctor.
>
> Scotland is developing its own legislation regarding this issue.

- private clubs. Where a club provides a service to people who are not members, they are covered by the act already and will have to make their services and premises accessible. Circumstances when this might be applicable include for example, a golf club which hires out a function room to the general public for wedding receptions or conventions.

Otherwise at present they are exempt from the DDA requirements, unless membership is open to any member of the public.

However, in the future, with the introduction of the Amendment Regulations, any club with 25 or more members will have to open their membership to people with disabilities and therefore make their services and goods available to them. They will not have to make physical changes to their buildings though (unless they provide other services to the public), only their policies and procedures for membership.

- manufacturers and designers in most cases do not provide services direct to the general public, and therefore do not have to make changes to their products, packaging or instructions. However, they will still need to ensure they follow the requirements of Parts 1 and 2 of the DDA and any guarantee system in place will have to abide by the part 3.1 and 3.2 rules

One other area has special rules under the provision of services part of the Disability Discrimination Act 1995 and that is insurance.

As insurance is a service it is covered under Part 3 of the DDA, but because insurance coverage is based upon risk, there can be some occasions where there is a good reason for charging more or putting into place certain restrictions for claiming.

However, there needs to be good evidence of a greater risk when giving the higher quote or putting more restrictions on the policy, and this needs to be based on facts not just someone's point of view.

When there is doubt over a reason for a higher price for a policy or the restrictions being put into place, then the Disability Rights Commission may be able to provide advice for the person with a disability involved or tell the insurance company where to go to consult a legally trained person.

Where the person with a disability is a member of a group looking for group insurance, a greater price or unreasonable restrictions cannot be placed on the policy.

Chapter Thirty-two: A Service Provider's duties and alterations that could be considered

From 1999 goods and service providers have had to change their practices, policies and procedures, and provide auxiliary (supplementary) aids and services. They have also had to provide their services by alternative means if their buildings are inaccessible.

Service providers can amend their policies so that you aren't excluded from using the services or accessing goods, and they can also provide disability awareness training to their staff so that they are better informed and less likely to discriminate.

The most well know examples of this type of change are:

- a shop or restaurant changing their policy of 'No Dogs Allowed' to 'Assistant Dogs Welcome'
- a nightclub changes their dress policy so that a person with a disability, which does not allow them to wear shoes, can wear trainers. This could be specifically done just for people with disabilities, so that the dress policy continues for non-disabled people
- a policy is changed so that all reception staff at a solicitor's are trained in disability awareness, deaf awareness and visual impairment awareness, which assists them in dealing with people with disabilities.

Auxiliary aids or services are usually specialist items of equipment or extra assistance for people with disabilities, which are over and above those normally provided.

For instance:

- a bank provides a hearing aid user with a portable loop system, in the form of a conference folder, during a meeting
- a lipspeaker is hired to interpret for a hard of hearing person attending a conference
- information is put onto audiotape for people with visual impairments
- new software is installed to assist people with mobility problems in using a computer in a library
- a supermarket provides a shop assistant to help a wheelchair user with their shopping
- a local authority provides a written bill to a customer, but includes a statement, which shows that large print, Braille and audiotape versions are available on request.

If a piece of equipment is purchased for use as an auxiliary aid, the service provider must ensure that it is available and in working order. If changes have been made that are not readily noticeable, the provider should advertise these through notices, such as loop signs where loops have been installed.

The following are a few more suggestions, which could be used by service providers to prevent discrimination:

- print information in plain English in a sans serif font (i.e a type face without legs) in a minimum of 12-point without using all capitalisation

- when necessary provide information in Braille, audiotape, large print, Moon, or video

- provide disability awareness training to all frontline staff such as receptionists, call staff and staff who meet and deal with members of the public

- ensure Assistant Dogs are allowed on the premises, and provide water if necessary for them – Guide Dogs for people with Visual Impairments are not the only dogs used for assistance. There are now hearing dogs for people with Hearing Impairments and assistant dogs for people with Physical Impairments

- provide meetings and conferences in accessible venues, such as on the ground floor, with loop systems in place, and with accessible toilets

- have a Textphone (Minicom) available for people with Hearing Impairments to contact, or train staff to use Typetalk a BT service for hearing people to use to contact people with hearing impairments and vice versa

- do not ask people with disabilities to sit in appropriate places to ease the discomfort of others. This especially applies to eating or drinking places

- train staff in deaf awareness and visual impairment awareness

- designate and train staff to take responsibility for evacuating people with disabilities in the event of a fire or emergency

- in the absence of a flashing fire alarm, provide vibrating pagers for people with hearing impairments to wear in the building if they are likely to be on their own anywhere – these are connected to the fire alarm system

- provide Evac-chairs to enable someone with a physical disability or medical condition affected by fire, smoke or stress, to get out in the event of a fire

- provide an interpreting service in meetings and conferences. This could be a lipspeaker, deaf/bind interpreter, or British Sign Language interpreter. However, interpreters are often hard to find and in great demand, so will need to be booked at least 2 weeks in advance if not longer. Also interpreters and clients will need breaks every 40 minutes or so during the meeting, and for very long meetings or conferences it is usual to book two interpreters who work in shifts

- if interpreters are not available because of an impromptu or emergency meeting then alternative means of communicating with the person with a hearing impairment must be discussed with them and used. This could be as simple as having to write everything down or using a computer

- provide portable loop systems in meetings and also at counters.

This list is not complete and there are many more examples quoted in the Code of Practice accompanying this Part of the Act.

Service providers must think about their policies and see if they actually make life difficult for a person with a disability. If so, the organisation must look to see how they can amend the policy to prevent the discrimination. When considering whether the service is difficult to the person with a disability to use, the provider should consider whether other people would consider the time, inconvenience, effort, discomfort or loss of dignity involved in using the service, unacceptable if they were experiencing similar difficulties.

If changes have had a cost, then service providers are usually not allowed to pass these charges onto you, unless there is a reason for it. For instance if a hotel has adapted several of its rooms to be accessible for a people with disabilities, then the price of those rooms cannot be more for the person with a disability than the other rooms for non-disabled people.

Sometimes there are good reasons for charging extra for a service, such as if it is a new and extra service provided by a company specifically for people with disabilities who cannot use the service any other way. This could be a shop that charges a delivery charge for sending shopping to the person's home as they cannot get to the shop themselves. As this is an extra, new, service it can be charged for as the service is not available to non-disabled people.

Therefore, if a service provider starts to provide a tailor made service to the person with a disability which is not provided to other people, the provider can charge more for the service.

Whatever a service and goods provider does initially to make sure that their services and goods are available to a person with a disability, their duties do not stop there. Providers will still need to monitor their changes and make more alterations in the future if they are needed. Advances in many areas may make the original alteration out of date, and new and better adjustments may become available. Providers will need to be aware of this and make the changes as they are required.

In most cases the changes that are required by goods and service providers do not need to cost a great deal, but can still benefit both the company and the clients with a disability.
The best idea before making changes is to consult with people with disabilities through local support groups or day centres.

There may even be a local access group, which can get involved in both the service provision and the changes to buildings. These groups can usually be accessed through the 'Access Officer' at your local council, and if you are interested in joining them, the Access Officer can tell you how to go about it.

People with disabilities and the Codes of Practice are the best sources of ideas as to how service providers can change and/or provide their services.

Chapter Thirty-three: Access to buildings and facilities

The Disability Discrimination Act 1995 states that services include the access to or use of any place or building, which allows member of the general public to use it. Therefore any person who allows the public to enter that place is proving a service to them and is subject to the rules of Part 3.3 of the Act.

From the 1 October 2004 where a physical feature of a building or place makes it impossible or extremely difficult for a person with a disability to use the services, the service provider will have to:

- remove the feature or
- alter it so that its not difficult to use anymore or
- provide a reasonable way of avoiding it or
- provide a reasonable method of providing the service (as in the service providers section above).

> Service providers should not automatically assume that the only way to make their services available to people with disabilities is to make a physical alteration to their buildings or premises. Quite often it is the changes in policies and procedures that are more likely to have a better effect, like training staff to take more time for people with disabilities or offering to help with shopping in the case of wheelchair user. Policies often prevent the need to change the fabric of the building without having to go to a lot of expense and time.

However, sometimes this isn't enough and the only answer is to either avoid the obstacle, or remove it.

Service providers should be able to identify the most obvious barriers for people with disabilities to get in and use their facilities or services, but the best and easiest way to ensure that a provider has recognised all the barriers is to actually ask the people with disabilities themselves.

> Most local authorities in the UK have an Access Officer and often an Access Group, which is made up of disabled people with a wide variety of backgrounds. They can advise on problems; sometimes carry out an access audit for the provider; and can suggest solutions for them

By listening carefully to these people, a service provider should be able to address any problems that they have come up against, so it is often worth talking to the owner or manager to discuss any issues you may have.

> It is worth remembering too that in making buildings and premises more accessible to people with disabilities, service providers are also opening up their service to parents with small children (double buggies being a good example) and older people, with even more spending opportunities.

Although the access to buildings part of the law doesn't come into effect until October 2004, service providers have been given plenty of time to prepare for its introduction, and there has been lots of information and advice available to them since the DDA became active in 1996.

It has made sense for providers to plan ahead, so that if they altered premises in the time period between the beginning of the law and the introduction of Part 3.3 in late 2004, they used this opportunity to make sure that they alter it to the benefit of people with disabilities. This period has meant to be a transitional period where people can prepare what they are going to do when it all becomes a legal requirement and there has been nothing stopping them from altering buildings before the deadline.

If anything were to happen to service providers in the future and you took them to court for not altering their premises, courts will be obliged to look at what they did prior to the Act coming into force and the time they had to prepare.

The law does not say exactly what people have to do to comply with the law, as long as what is done is successful in removing the barriers to the services for people with disabilities. What the law sasy is important is that the barriers are removed and if a service provider does not do everything in their power to do this, then they may have to defend their decisions.

For example if a service provider puts a policy into place which effectively removes the obstacles and a person with a disability can now access the services without any problems, then that will be enough to comply with the law. If the policy still doesn't do enough to allow that person to use the services, the service provider may have to do more and if they can't, then they may have to justify why they can't.

In some circumstances this may be related to the cost, but if nothing at all is done, including not investigating possibilities, they will be responsible under the law and could face legal action.

However, removing or altering barriers created by physical features of a building is a comprehensive way of making the services available to everyone. By just altering a policy, people with disabilities can be offered the same services but not in the same manner as everyone else, which can still make a person with disabilities feel as though they are being treated differently.

The removal of physical barriers may seem like an expensive option but in the long run may turn out to be cheaper than having to continue to provide alternative services or policies, such as those which are labour intensive, and will expand the number of customers too.

Therefore, service providers are encouraged to look at the physical things first, and if it isn't reasonable to remove or avoid them, then look at other ways of providing the service. A good start to doing this is to have an access audit done.

> An access audit looks at all the physical features of a building including signage, loop systems, fire alarms, where items are stored, lighting and all the other more obvious items such as doors, corridors, toilets, and so on. It then details the findings and any problems in a report, often with suggestions on how to overcome them as well.

Making a plan to alter the items which have been found in an audit, and acting on these as time and money allow, will usually be seen favourably by people with disabilities and courts.

The DDA described physical features, whether temporary or permanent, as:

- any feature arising from the design or construction of a building on the premises occupied by a service provider
- any feature on those premises, or any approach to, exit from or access to such a building
- any fixtures and fittings, furnishings, furniture, equipment or materials in or on such premises
- any of the above bought onto the premises by or on behalf of the service provider in the course of and for the purpose of providing services to the public
- any other physical element or quality of land comprised in the premises occupied by the service provider.

The following examples are all classed as physical features and can be made more accessible:

Steps and stairs – need to be the same height and width, have handrails and have the edges marked.

Kerbs – some kerbs are deliberately high at bus stops to assist the new buses, but where a road can be crossed, the kerb should be dropped, and if necessary tactile or bumpy paving put in to tell people with visual impairments where the edge of the pavement is.

Parking spaces – should be near to the service providers building, wide enough to allow people to get in and out easily and have dropped kerb to let people get onto the pavement.

Pavements – should be even, wide enough to get two people past, and unobstructed by shopware.

Entrances – should be easy to get through without revolving doors.

Exits – should be easy to get out of.

Fire escapes – should be easy to get out of in an emergency so without ridges at the bottom, or be too stiff to open.

Ramps – shouldn't be too steep and should always have a flat area at the top or at regular intervals if it is long.

Internal doors – should be easy to open and have glass in them so that you can see people behind it, and a metal strip along the bottom so that wheelchair users don't put their footrests through it.

Corridors and aisles – should be clear of clutter to allow people to walk through easily.

Toilets, washing facilities and showers – should be accessible to people with disabilities only and not become changing rooms for non-disabled parents and their children.

Telephones – should be at a reasonable height with a chair and a shelf.

Reception desks and service counters – should have one area that is low enough for wheelchair user to see over.

Lighting – switches should be lowered so that people can reach them easily and the lighting never flickering.

Lifts – should talk and have a readable display if it goes more than one floor, so that people with visual impairments and hearing impairments know where they are, and in the event of an emergency, know how to get help.

Floor covering – should be non-slippy or low pile and even, so that wheelchair users can cross easily.

Door handles – large handles at a low height are required which are easy to open.

Security – doorbells, pads, locks, cameras, fire 'break-glass' systems and alarms – all at a lower height and in full working order at all times.

These examples are covered in more detail in Part M legislation (see guidance section), which is discussed below.

Other items covered include:

- signage, including display screens
- bollards
- bus-stops
- acoustics (noise levels, echoes and so on)
- tables and chairs
- seating
- paths – plants and trees can obstruct, the path can be too narrow or steep.
- display racks
- escalators
- any other item that could be considered a physical feature.

Where a problem occurs that is not on actual premises such as pavements, kerbs, bollards, and any other road or pavement object, the Highway Authority is the service provider and should be contacted. This could be a Local Authority's responsibility or even the National Highways Agency in which case the Local Authority can point you the in right direction.

> A service provider may have to get consent from the local council or national governing body (such as the National Trust for listed buildings) before they make any changes to the premises. These could include planning permission, building regulations approval or a building warrant in Scotland, listed building consent, scheduled monument consent and fire regulation approval.
>
> Service Providers should plan and predict the need to obtain this planning consent to make an alteration to their buildings or premises, which can take time.
>
> During this waiting time it would be reasonable for the service provider to look at other ways of making their services accessible, which could include changing policies or procedures as discussed before, but they must ensure that your dignity is not jeopardised in any way by doing this.
>
> The Act does not allow people to change their premises or buildings without the relevant consent.

Approved Document Part M & M1 are the builder's regulations governing how they make buildings accessible to people with disabilities, and every building whether being built now or being refurbished in England and Wales should meet the requirements of this guidance. Following these rules will make the building or premise safe and convenient for people with disabilities to get into the place and move around it.

However, the Part M & M1 regulations may not cover all the requirements of the DDA, and more alterations may need to be completed to bring it in line with the legislation.

However, any alteration, which met with part M approval before the 2004 deadline, will have ten years from when the modification took place to amend the alteration again to meet the requirements of the DDA.

> For example a bank altered its internal doors to Part M requirements in 1999 – it will not have to alter them again until 2009, and then only if they have been found to be too small under the new regulations or if a person has requested they be changed because they are not adequately wide enough for them. But the service provider will have to make either a reasonable way of avoiding the doorways or an alternative method of the disabled person in question of using the services provided by the bank.

Nevertheless, if they alter them again in the time before 2009 they will have to comply this time.

Service providers will have to also consider the physical aspects that are not covered by Part M such as car parking facilities (controlling blue badge spaces), signage, and loop systems.

Sometimes buildings are shared by many service providers, and although they may lease separate parts of a building, there may be areas that the public use, which is useful to all the paying tenants. For example a shopping precinct, which has toilets, entrance halls, stairways and lifts.

In these cases the Disability Discrimination Act does not specify whether they are the responsibility of the landlord or the tenant, but generally speaking if the area is one that the landlord allows members of the general public to use, it will be up to the owner to make the changes.

Service providers are asked to consider the difficulties people with disabilities would encounter in trying to use their services in a particular building, and if this look as though it could be costly, they may want to look at other venues for their business.

When can goods and service providers justify discrimination against a person with a disability?

In every situation a service provider should not be looking for reasons or excuses to discriminate against people with disabilities as it is in their own best interests to make sure that their services are available to everyone.

Sometimes there are genuine reasons for not complying with the Disability Discrimination Act, but these are few and far between, and service providers should normally consult a professional before making the decision not to change the way a service is provided or the premises they being provided from.

Most health and safety issues can be overcome through changes in policies or providing other equipment or training that would help and generally fire safety cannot be used as a good reason for not doing something.

If a service provider will not be able to provide the service to anyone else because of the changes it would have to make to enable you to use it, they would not be made to change.

Or if by providing the service differently the provider would effective change the service completely, the provider will not have to make the change.

Or if by providing the service differently the provider would face severe financial problems, they will not have to make the changes.

Chapter Thirty-four: Education Law – Special Educational Needs and Disability Act 2001 (SENDA)

The area of education has its own legislation, the Special Educational Needs and Disability Act 2001 (SENDA) which amends the requirements of the Disability Discrimination Act 1995.

The only requirement for schools, and post 16 education and related services, regarding the provision of education under Part 4 of the DDA is that they have to provide their information in an accessible format for people with disabilities. Where they provide a service to members of the public, they will become service providers and have to follows the rules governing access to goods, services and facilities.

SENDA makes it against the law to discriminate against disabled candidates, potential students or actual students with disabilities. It uses the DDA definition of a person with a disability, but defines a student as being anyone under 16 or over 16, in full time and part time education, postgraduates, undergraduates, students from the UK and those from abroad, students on short courses, day schools, evening classes, taster courses, or a modular section of a course or anyone visiting from another education organization.

Candidates and potential students include people who attend open days, interviews, receive a prospectus or who are targeted by recruitment drives.

The organisations which are involved in this section of the Act and SENDA are:

- higher and further education agencies

- further education colleges in Scotland
- Local Education Authorities (LEAs) including adult and community education schools
- LEAs providing statutory youth and community services.

Private providers of education and work-based training, non-statutory youth services, activities provided by voluntary agencies, scouts, or church youth groups, are not covered by the Act, but are covered under Part 3 of the Act because they are classed as a service.

All the following areas are also considered as activities organised by an education facility and therefore have to be subjected to the rules of the law too:

- ectures
- practical lessons
- field trips and outing
- work placements
- distance learning
- internet courses
- exams
- assessments.

Finally all the following are services provided by the education organisation, which are covered by the DDA Part 4 and SENDA:

- libraries
- computer facilities

- counselling services
- catering
- residential facilities
- leisure facilities
- buildings
- equipment
- grounds
- welfare and financial services
- careers services
- medical services
- religious services
- recreation and entertainment facilities
- childcare
- parking
- shops
- graduation and other ceremonies.

It doesn't matter if the service is provided by someone other than the education facility, as they are still responsible under this part of the Act in ensuring discrimination does not occur.

As with the other areas of the DDA, Part 4 states that discrimination against candidates, potential students and students with disabilities can occur by:

- treating them less favourably than non-disabled people
- failing to make reasonable adjustments for them.

Anything that can make your life easier as a candidate, potential student or an actual student is classed as a reasonable adjustment. This could involve:

- providing equipment to assist with the learning or delivery of teaching.
- changing a policy
- providing material in an accessible format for you.
- providing an interpreter for you.
- training wtaff to make them aware of how to work with you, and how to go about making changes to assist you
- altering the physical aspects of buildings.

Educational organisations also have to anticipate the changes they must make so that students with disabilities can make use of their training facilities and other services provided. This might mean that the institution has to consult with people with disabilities and have access audits undertaken in order to prepare for the changes they need to make.

Part 4 comes into force in various stages.

Most of it is already in place and has been since September 2002. The requirements for making adjustments came into force in 2003 and the finally part about changing buildings such as described in Part 3 (Access to buildings and facilities) comes into force for education establishments in September 2005.

Organisations are only expected to do what is reasonable for them to do, which depends upon the individual circumstances of the case including how important the service or change is and whether it will make a big difference for the person with a disability and whether there are enough resources to do what is required.

Other things to be considered when looking at making changes are how much the changes will impact upon other students, including their studies and whether health and safety will be compromised in any way.

In the end if you are looking at becoming a student or are already a student, you may wish to discuss changes in the way courses are run; equipment that may help you with the course; how other services being provided could be altered to help you; or how buildings could be changed to make your life easier with your course tutor or other staff member.

Chapter Thirty-five: The Disability Rights Commission; duties and practice

The Disability Discrimination Act 1995 established a new independent organisation, the National Disability Council (NDC), which covered England, Scotland and Wales and it also established the Northern Ireland Disability Council. Both these bodies were there to advise the Government about disability issues and how the new Act should be put into practice.

Then in 1997, the Government established another group, with the backing of the NDC, called the Disability Rights Task Force, who would undertake a wide consultation exercise on how to start the process of introducing the enforceable sections of the law.

At this time the government also said that it would continue to implement the rest of the Act at the times it had agreed, but that they would look at getting a Disability Rights Commission (DRC) set up to oversee disability issues and provide information and advice where necessary.

This would be an independent body, made up of paid workers, a Chief Executive and a Board of Directors, backed up by a Minister for Disabilities.

So in 1998 the Disability Rights Task Force and the Government set out its proposals for the Commission, including its roles and functions, in a White Paper Consultation document. This was available to all the disability organisations and the general public, who all had the chance to comment and suggest amendments to how the DRC would work.

The response to this consultation paper, showed that there was generally a lot of support from across the country for a DRC, and the Government went ahead an introduced the Disability Rights

Commission Bill in the House of Lords later that year, and the House of Commons early the following year.

Parliament agreed with the ideas laid out in the Act and the Bill to set the DRC up was passed in July 1999, and became a law.

Finally in April 2000, the Disability Rights Commission opened for business and the National Disability Council and Disability Rights Task Group closed.

Duties

The Disability Rights Commission has published it goal as having 'a society where all disabled people can participate fully as equal citizens'. And there are duties on the Commission.

These are:

- to work to eliminate discrimination against people with disabilities
- to promote equal opportunities for people with disabilities
- to encourage good practice in the social treatment of people with disabilities
- to advise the Government on how the DDA 1995 and DRC Act 1999 are working.

Who can the DRC help?

The Commission will answer questions from any member of the public, employers or any other service with 249 or less employees. It can't answer questions about benefits, community care, equipment for people with disabilities, housing or medical treatment.

Neither can they give advice to service providers, employers, schools or further education facilities with regard to specific issues with a person with disabilities who has made a complaint or for whom they are making reasonable adjustments.

The reason for this is that the disabled person in question may need the help of the DRC about the issue, and the Commission's first duty is to assist that person with their rights under the DDA 1995.

The DRC can tell these organisations where to go to get appropriate help in these circumstances.

Other professions that cannot be helped by staff at the Disability Rights Commission include solicitors or barristers, as employees of the DRC are not legally trained.

Employers with 250 or more employees are regarded as being in a position to get legal help on their own, and therefore the DRC are not in a position to assist. However, these organisations are able to access the DRC's publications, which may provide some help. The DRC services are there to assist individuals and small businesses that may not have any other sources of advice and information about the DDA 1995 or Amendment Regulations 2003.

What the DRC has to do

The DRC has a number of specific tasks that they have to carry out to make sure that they are meeting their duties.

These are:

1. Assistance

The Disability Rights Commission can help people with disabilities when they feel they have been discriminated against. They can arrange legal advice for that person or representation and in some circumstances can even help you take someone to court. These instances are usually when a case raises a matter of principle or if it would be unreasonable to deal with the case unaided. By taking people to court when they have broken the DDA law, the DRC are testing the limits of the law by means of helping to identify instances of discrimination and stop the same things happening again.

They also offer support to help to solve problems without going to court or employment tribunal, and in certain circumstances they will refer your case to the Disability Conciliation Service (see below).

2. Information and Advice

The DRC have to provide advice and information to the general public, employers and service providers about their rights and duties under the DDA 1995. This comes in several forms, the first being through leaflets and booklets outlining specific things people have to do to meet the law requirements and secondly through a helpline or e-mail via the internet.

When a person contacts the helpline, an advisor will answer the call. If you have a question about the DDA 1995 or Amendment Regulations 2003, or you think that you may have been discriminated against in some way, your call will be transferred to a specialist advisor.

All calls are recorded so that the DRC can monitor how well they are doing and if a complaint is made they can investigate the call.

If a non-disabled person contacts the DRC helpline for advice or information on behalf of a person with disabilities, the DRC cannot take any personal details about the disabled person, or take further action unless they have specific written consent from that person. However, if that person with a disability is unable to give written or verbal consent because of their disability, the DRC will make an alteration to the rule and ignore this requirement.

3. Codes of Practice

The Commission has to prepare and review Codes of Practice, which provide practical advice to people with disabilities, employers and service providers. This advice should help people meet their requirements under the Act and give examples of good practice.

Although these Codes may not give all the examples of things that can be done to ensure non-discriminatory practice against people with disabilities, if people have followed them it should demonstrate that the organisation is trying to meet their requirements. However, the best policy is always to consult the person with a disability who is involved about the changes that are best for them. If someone fails to obey any provision in the Codes of Practice they may not have take legal action taken against them, but a Court or Employment Tribunal will take into account any condition of a Code which it considers relevant to the case.

Any Code of Practice produced by the Disability Rights Commission must be approved by the Secretary of State and shown to the Government in Parliament.

4. Conciliation

The DRC provides an independent mediation service through Mediation UK that helps in the event of disagreements between people with disabilities and service providers over access to goods and services. The Commission also monitors the effectiveness of this service.

If a person with a disability feels that they have a case against someone who provides goods and services, or access to education, the Conciliation service at the DRC may be able to help. This service is free of charge, funded by the DRC, and they aim to find a solution that satisfies both you and the business involved. Most of the time businesses and organisations are will to reach a discussed settlement, which will show them in a more favourable way.

The DRC take referrals for this service, as they have to check that there is a legal basis for the case and that conciliation is the best way forward. If mediation doesn't work then the person with a disability still has the right to take the person concerned to court.

5. Investigations

The DRC can carry out formal investigations into how people with disabilities are treated in specific organisations or different sectors of business, including possible unlawful acts by particular bodies. If found to have breached the law, the DRC can issue notices or agreements or if continuing to act unlawfully, provide assistance to take the organisation to court. The DRC has the power to get any person to give written or oral information relating to an investigation being carried out.

If the Commission has carried out an investigation and found that someone either has committed or is committing something, which is contrary to the DDA, it may issue a Non-Discrimination Notice, which can take one or two forms:

A Non-discrimination Notice will always give details of the unlawful activity and inform that it must cease.

It may also require the person to produce an action plan to show how they are going to avoid the unlawful activity in the future. If this action plan is not good enough, then the DRC are able to go to court to apply for an Order to restrain them from discriminatory activity. (Failing to comply with an Order may result in a fine).

If the Commission feels that a Non-Discrimination Notice is not necessary, but that changes still need to be made, they may enter into an agreement with the person whom it believes has committed an unlawful act.

This contract between the Commission and the person involved outlines the agreement that the person will not commit any more unlawful acts of the same kind, and the DRC agrees not to take any further action against them. The agreement may also specify any other action that the DRC feel is relevant for the person involved. This could be something as simple as requiring them to attend a disability awareness course, or rather more complex such as changes policies and procedures.

If the other person involved in the agreement fails to obey the terms of the contract, and persistently discriminates in the same way, then the DRC can apply to the courts for an order along the same lines as the non-discriminatory notices.

Chapter Thirty-six: Disability awareness checklist for employers and service providers

People with disabilities are people first and foremost and not people suffering from a medical condition or disability. It is always paramount to ask the person with a disability what would be best for them, rather than assume you know and understand the barriers they may be facing.

Also many disabilities are hidden – you can't see them. So in these instances if they tell you they have a disability you will have to believe them, and make the changes they need.

It is always worth getting a disability audit done professionally, because they may see things that you don't and be able to think laterally to come up with solutions to the problems.

Always try to plan ahead so that expenses don't add up over time. If you are refurbishing now, then the Disability Discrimination Act should be met when you are doing it or you'll have to do it again in the future.

Staff should always be kept informed of any changes, and generally would benefit from disability awareness training. There are some courses, which can be taken across the Internet, or at work through workbooks, as well as having day courses involving staff being away from their workplace.

Consider the details of a job and the personal specification, and make sure that these are very specific to the job.

If there are health considerations for a job then you need to justify these. Similarly if there are health considerations for not altering service provision the reasons will need to be acceptable.

Think!

- Can I do anything that would assist this person to use my service?
- Is there anything I do now which would make it difficult for this person to use my service?
- If so, what can I do to change it?
- Always talk to the person with a disability – never their carer or person with them.
- Always focus on a person's abilities, not their disabilities.
- Make sure that you have an equal opportunities policy and that staff all know and abide by it.
- Review all your policies to make sure that they aren't discriminating in any way.
- Always introduce yourself to a blind person – they may not know you are there, or will know someone's there but not whom. Also tell them if you leave or they might end up talking to the air.
- Never lean on a wheelchair, but always try to talk to the wheelchair user at their level.
- If a sign language interpreter is present assisting a deaf person always speak directly to the deaf person, and look at them at all times, they may lip-read as well.
- Don't loose patience with people, especially those with speech problems or those with learning difficulties.
- Don't stare, and don't ask personal questions about the person's disability.
- Assistance dogs are usually working when they are out, so they should never be touched without the owner's permission.
- You can offer assistance to a person with a disability but you must wait for them to accept it before actually helping them out.

Part Four: Some common issues
Neil Bateman

Chapter Thirty-seven: Community Care services

The term Community Care refers to the provision of social care services by local authorities to people with a disability or older people. These include services to keep people living independently as well as residential care services. Community Care Services are provided by Social Services Departments in England and Wales and Social Work Departments in Scotland, but increasingly services are being provided jointly by local authorities and the National Health Service or by private bodies under contract to them.

A full explanation of these services is beyond the scope of this book, however, local authorities have powers to provide services which can help people with a disability to access work, training or education and some of these are explained here. You should consult The Disability Alliance's Disability Rights Handbook and Child Poverty Action Group's Paying for Care Handbook for more information.

In order to access any Community Care Services, you will normally have to meet the Eligibility Criteria for services. In England, these are set down in guidance from the Department of Health known as Fair Access to Care Services and contain four levels of need. Local authorities have to operate the criteria but can decide, within reason, to only allow access at certain levels. This discretion must be exercised consistently and fairly and after consulting disabled people and their carers.

Before accessing most services, you should have a Community Care Assessment which involves you being consulted about your needs and the type of services you need. You should also receive an explanation about any charges which you may have to pay.

The assessment will then be used to make a Care Plan, this should be in writing and you should receive a copy of it. Services you won't need a Community Care Assessment for are those such as Disabled Person's Parking Permits (Blue Badges – formerly known as Orange Badges) and information and advice.

If you are a disabled young person, a Community Care Assessment may happen as part of the transition planning which is undertaken to help you move on from education or into higher or further education.

The quality, range and availability of services vary hugely between local authorities. However, local authorities have duties or powers to provide the following services which are connected with work, training and education:

- employment in sheltered workshops
- life skills and other training at day centres for people with a disability
- community support staff to help you negotiate the maze of public services and help you to access services
- home care services to help with personal care and practical tasks at home
- telephones and emergency alarms
- transport to day centres and workshops
- equipment to help you remain independent and advice from an occupational therapist to develop self-care and independent living skills.

If you are assessed as requiring a particular service, the local authority cannot restrict access to this because it has insufficient resources. However, it can limit how it operates the eligibility criteria if it does not have sufficient resources.

If you are a carer, you have the right to have a separate carer's assessment. This looks at the support you need to continue as caring and should take account of any work, education or training you are undertaking.

Charges (not Scotland)

You may be asked to pay a charge for certain services. Charges for residential care are laid down by government. If you are a less dependant resident, the local authority has discretion to waive or reduce charges. They also have discretion to not charge for short-stays in care.

Most local authorities make charges for services in your home. There are certain rules in government guidance about this:

- if you have a partner, your partner's resources must be ignored unless they also receive a service
- if you receive Income Support or Pension Credit, no charge can be made against this except for the severe disability premium or the equivalent severe disability extra amount in Pension Credit
- if a charge is to be levied against your Disability Living Allowance or Attendance Allowance or the severe disability premium, an assessment of your disability related costs must be carried out.

If you cannot afford to pay a charge for a service provided to you in your home, the local authority have discretion to reduce or waive the charge if it is not reasonably practicable for you to pay it.

The local authority is not allowed to stop a service if you don't pay your charges. If you are unhappy with the charge or can't afford it you can make a formal complaint and ultimately have a hearing before a Complaints Panel. After this you may take legal action known as Judicial Review or make a complaint to the Local Government Ombudsman.

Services provided to help you move out of hospital (known as Intermediate Care) must not be charged for until after they have been provided for six weeks.

Chapter Thirty-eight: Going into hospital

During a stay in hospital (or a similar institution) where someone receives care paid for by the National Health Service, social security benefits may be reduced or stopped. Until 21 May 2003, most benefits were affected after six weeks but they are now affected after 52 weeks.

However, Disability Living and Attendance Allowances continue to be affected after 28 days in hospital and Carer's Allowance at 12 weeks. This means that people on means-tested benefits who have been receiving additional amounts in their applicable amount because they also receive AA or DLA will receive a lower amount after 28 days in hospital. Short stays in hospital which are less than 28 days apart are added together to decide when the reduction of benefit should start. So two periods of 21 days in hospital with a week apart add up to 42 in hospital.

If the person being cared for is in hospital, the carer's Carer's Allowance will stop when Attendance Allowance or Disability Living Allowance stops. However, any carer's premium in the means tested benefit will continue for a further eight weeks.

People who are in hospital on a long-term basis and whose benefit has been reduced or stopped, can have it increased for short stays outside hospital.

If the person receives benefits which are affected by a hospital stay, it is important to notify the DWP office which pays them, just before they reach the point when the benefit is affected. Notification will avoid overpayments of benefit (which are likely to be recoverable). Similarly when someone whose benefit has been reduced, has a date to leave hospital, it is important to quickly notify all the offices paying benefits so that these can be increased to the correct level, thus helping speed up discharge. This is particularly so for Attendance and Disability Living Allowances because passported higher amounts of means-tested benefits may be payable. A person may also qualify for a

Social Fund Community Care Grant to help them go home or to prevent re-admission.

People on Jobseeker's Allowance (JSA) can be sick for up to two weeks a year (or in a jobseeking period if under a year) without having to make a claim for Incapacity Benefit. If someone on JSA does go into hospital, it will be particularly important to notify Jobcentre Plus immediately in order to avoid disruption to their payment.

Of course, a stay in hospital may be a useful trigger to review whether or not someone is receiving all the benefits they are entitled to.

The following benefits are not normally affected by a stay in hospital:

- Tax Credits (but if an award runs out during a hospital stay, the requirement to be in work for 16 hours a week may not be satisfied)
- Industrial Disablement Benefit, Maternity Allowance
- Statutory Maternity Pay, Statutory Adoption Pay, Statutory Paternity Pay, and Statutory Sick Pay
- Child Benefit (but see below).

When a child is in hospital, any benefits paid for them stop at 12 weeks unless expenditure is being regularly incurred for the child (e.g. on the cost of visits and gifts). However, this does not apply to a child's Disability Living Allowance. For Child Benefit, the expenditure should be at least at the same amount as the benefit.

If people find that their Housing or Council Tax Benefits reduce or are insufficient when they have been in hospital (for example, they have rent arrears) they can apply for a Discretionary Housing Payment. This can also be helpful if other income has reduced.

Benefits paid to people who are in hospices or hospitals not provided nor paid for by the NHS are unaffected.

The issue of hospitalisation and benefits is quite complex, so specialist advice is often helpful.

Going into hospital – the effect on benefits

Benefit	After 28 days	After 12 weeks	After 52 weeks
Attendance Allowance, Constant Attendance Allowance & Disability Living Allowance	Stops after 28 days in hospital if the claimant is aged 16 or older. But if under 16, it is payable for up to 12 weeks. Payable for any time spent outside hospital.	Not payable	Not payable
Income Support	Severe disability premium stops when AA/DLA stops	Carer's premium continues for eight weeks after Carer's Allowance stops	*Single person:* IS applicable amount reduces to £15.90 and no housing costs *Couple, one in hospital:* both treated as single people. Partner in hospital gets £15.90 and partner at home gets IS as a single person *Single parent:* gets £19.90 unless is no longer responsible for children when applicable amount is reduced to £15.90
Housing and Council Tax Benefits	Severe disability premium stops when AA/DLA stops	Carer's premium continues for 8 weeks after Carer's Allowance stops	HB not payable but CTB may continue if absence is unlikely to substantially exceed 52 weeks. Discount on Council Tax may be possible The 52 week period restarts if they spend any time at home
Pension Credit	Severe disability element stops when AA/DLA stops	Carer's element continues for eight weeks after Carer's Allowance stops	*Single person:* standard minimum guarantee reduces to £15.90. *Couples:* have to claim separately if absence likely to substantially exceed 52 weeks
Carer's Allowance		Stops. Carer's premium continues for eight more weeks	
Retirement Pension, Bereavement Benefits & Incapacity Benefit			If no dependant's addition being paid, benefit reduced to £15.90. If there is a dependant, the balance of the benefit less £30.24 is paid to dependant. Dependant may need to claim means tested benefits in their own right

Chapter Thirty-nine: Benefits and residential Care

When a person moves into a residential care or nursing home (either temporarily or permanently) there may be effects on some of their benefits. It is particularly important to maximise benefit take-up when people live in residential care as this will help pay fees and if people are placed by a local authority (or Health Board in Northern Ireland), the benefits will increase income from charges. The rules about benefits and charges for people who live in residential care are complex and full details are in Child Poverty Action Group's Paying for Care Handbook.

It is important that responsibility for paying for care – local authority or National Health Service is clarified and there have been many situations when free care should have been provided by the NHS (though they will receive benefits as if they were hospital in-patients), but instead have been subjected to local authority charges. People who have been in hospital compulsorily under some Sections of the Mental Health Act 1983 and who then have residential care provided or arranged by a local authority as part of their aftercare under Section 117 of that Act cannot be charged. Similarly, the first six weeks of any intermediate care package must be free. If in any doubt, seek advice.

People aged 60 or over in residential care are entitled to Pension Credit and this is assessed using the normal rules.

Couples in residential care should usually be treated as two single people for benefit purposes – seek advice if they are treated as a couple.

Social Services Department can charge for any permanent residential care (but for a temporary stay, there is discretion not to charge and in Scotland there is no charge for care services, though people have to pay for accommodation and living costs. For temporary care, there is discretion about charges.

Some benefit income is ignored:

- Attendance Allowance
- Disability Living Allowance
- £10 of a War Pension
- £4.65 of any Pension Credit savings credit (£6.95 for a couple).

Anyone with capital above £20,000 is liable for the full cost of their care with tariff income being assumed from capital between £12,250 and £19,999.

The charge will also be reduced if it includes nursing care – an assessment of how much care someone needs is made and there are three bands.

The charge for permanent care should leave at least £18.10 a week (£18.40 in Wales) for personal expenses. There is also discretion to allow a higher amount for personal expenses. If someone is a less dependent resident, the local authority has discretion to vary charges favourably.

Benefits and residential care – a brief outline guide

All benefits are unaffected in residential care except for those in the table. This is a summary of the main rules but there are some exceptions.

Benefits	Temporary care	Permanent care
Attendance Allowance	Stops of 28 days (including short periods separated by less than a 29 day gap), unless person is meeting the full cost of care.	Same as temporary care
Disability Living Allowance (care component only)	Stops of 28 days (including short periods separated by less than a 29 day gap), unless person is meeting the full cost of care.	Same as temporary care
Income Support	Normal IS rules apply for up to 13 weeks. Couples 'disaggregated' and treated as two single people.	Normal rules apply in independent homes but if in a local authority home, Part III rate paid of which £18.10 is for 'personal expenses'.
Pension Credit	Normal rates paid except any amount for severe disability; stops when AA/DLA care stops. Couples treated as couples.	Normal rates paid except any amount for severe disability; stops when AA/DLA care stops. Lower capital limit increased to £10,000. Couples treated as two single people.
Housing Benefit	May continue on main home in the community for up to 13 weeks or 52 weeks in some cases.	Not payable unless having a trial period and retain rent liability for home in the community. May be paid for up to four weeks after a stay becomes permanent. HB can't be paid towards the cost of residential care.
Council Tax Benefit	Payable for any Council Tax due on the home in the community.	Not payable unless having a trial period and have a Council Tax liability on home in the community. May qualify for a reduction/discount in Council Tax liability.

Chapter Forty: Energy efficiency grants

Grants to help with energy efficiency thus helping reduce fuel poverty and global warming are available. There are slightly different amounts and eligibility in England, Wales, Scotland and Northern Ireland.

If you receive a means tested benefit or maximum Tax Credit or you receive a disability related benefit you may qualify.

For more information contact:

- England (Eastern, East Midland, Yorkshire and Humber regions) 0800 952 0600
- England (other regions) 0800 316 2808
- Scotland 0800 072 0150
- Wales 0800 316 2815
- Northern Ireland 0800 181 667.

Important issues

- the scope of these grants has been significantly increased since 2000. Many people may be unaware that they could now receive help
- Tax Credits have brought more people into possible entitlement – particularly people without children
- people who had a grant under the previous and more limited Home Energy Efficiency Scheme may not realise that they may now qualify for a grant under the new scheme

- it is also worth exploring the possibility of a Home Repair Assistance grant from a local authority. These are discretionary grants for householders on low-income benefits or who are disabled or who are aged 60 or over. The scope of these grants varies

- the different schemes in the UK arise because they are included in the powers of the devolved administrations.

Further information and guidance

Personal Capability Assessment (PCA) Indicators

Physical disabilities

Activity	Descriptor	Points
1. Walking on level ground with a walking stick or other aid if such is normally used	(a) Cannot walk at all	15
	(b) Cannot walk more than a few steps without stopping or severe discomfort	15
	(c) Cannot walk more than 50 metres without stopping or severe discomfort	15
	(d) Cannot walk more than 200 metres without stopping or severe discomfort	7
	(e) Cannot walk more than 400 metres without stopping or severe discomfort	3
	(f) Cannot walk more than 800 metres without stopping or severe discomfort	0
	(g) No walking problem	0
2. Walking up and down stairs	(a) Cannot walk up and down one stair	15
	(b) Cannot walk up and down a flight of 12 stairs	15
	(c) Cannot walk up and down a flight of 12 stairs without holding on and taking rest	7
	(d) Cannot walk up and down a flight of 12 stairs without holding on	3
	(e) Can only walk up and down a flight of 12 stairs if he goes sideways or one step at a time	3
	(f) No problem in walking up and down stairs	0
3. Sitting in an upright chair with a back, but no arms	(a) Cannot sit comfortably	15
	(b) Cannot sit comfortably for more than 10 minutes without having to move from the chair because the degree of discomfort makes it impossible to continue sitting	15

Activity	Descriptor	Points
3. (continued)	(c) Cannot sit comfortably for more than 30 minutes without having to move from the chair because the degree of discomfort makes it impossible to continue sitting	15
	(d) Cannot sit comfortably for more than 1 hour without having to move from the chair because the degree of discomfort makes it impossible to continue sitting	7
	(e) Cannot sit comfortably for more than 2 hours without having to move from the chair because the degree of discomfort makes it impossible to continue sitting	3
	(f) No problem with sitting	0
4. Standing without the support of another person or the use of an aid except a walking stick	(a) Cannot stand unassisted	15
	(b) Cannot stand for more than a minute before needing to sit down	15
	(c) Cannot stand for more than 10 minutes before needing to sit down	15
	(d) Cannot stand for more than 30 minutes before needing to sit down	7
	(e) Cannot stand for more than 10 minutes before needing to move around	7
	(f) Cannot stand for more than 30 minutes before needing to move around	3
	(g) No problem standing	0
5. Rising from sitting in an upright chair with a back but no arms without the help of another person	(a) Cannot rise from sitting to standing	15
	(b) Cannot rise from sitting to standing without holding on to something	7
	(c) Sometimes cannot rise from sitting to standing without holding onto something	3
	(d) No problem with rising from sitting to standing	0
6. Bending and kneeling	(a) Cannot bend to touch knees and straighten up again	15

Activity	Descriptor	Points
6. (continued)	(b) Cannot either bend or kneel, or bend and kneel as if to pick up a piece of paper from the floor and straighten up again	7
	(c) Sometimes cannot either bend or kneel, or bend and kneel as if to pick up a piece of paper from the floor and straighten up again	3
	(d) No problem with bending and kneeling	0
7. Manual dexterity	(a) Cannot turn the pages of a book with either hand	15
	(b) Cannot turn a sink tap or the control knobs on a cooker with either hand	15
	(c) Cannot pick up a coin which is 2.5 centimetres or less in diameter with either hand	15
	(d) Cannot use a pen or pencil	15
	(e) Cannot tie a bow in laces or string	10
	(f) Cannot turn a sink tap or the control knobs on a cooker with one hand but can with the other	6
8. Lifting and carrying by use of the upper body and arms (excluding all other activities in Part 1 of the Assessment)	(a) Cannot pick up a paperback book with either hand	15
	(b) Cannot pick up and carry a 0.5 litre carton of milk with either hand	15
	(c) Cannot pick up and pour from a full saucepan or kettle of 1.7 litre capacity with either hand	15
	(d) Cannot pick up and carry a 2.5 kilogram bag of potatoes with either hand	8
	(e) Cannot pick up and carry a 0.5 litre carton of milk with one hand, but can with the other	6
	(f) Cannot pick up and carry a 2.5 kilogram bag of potatoes	0
9. Reaching	(a) Cannot raise either arm as if to put something in the top pocket of a coat or jacket	15

Activity	Descriptor	Points
9. (continued)	(b) Cannot raise either arm to head as if to put on a hat	15
	(c) Cannot put either arm behind back as if to put on a coat or jacket	15
	(d) Cannot raise either arm above head as if to reach for something	15
	(e) Cannot raise one arm to head as if to put on a hat, but can with the other	6
	(f) Cannot raise one arm above head as if to reach for something but can with the other	0
	(g) No problem with reaching	0
10. Speech	(a) Cannot speak	15
	(b) Speech cannot be understood by family or friends	15
	(c) Speech cannot be understood by strangers	15
	(d) Strangers have great difficulty understanding speech	10
	(e) Strangers have some difficulty understanding speech	8
	(f) No problems with speech	0
11. Hearing with a hearing aid or other aid if normally worn.	(a) Cannot hear sounds at all	15
	(b) Cannot hear well enough to follow a television programme with the volume turned up	15
	(c) Cannot hear well enough to understand someone talking in a loud voice in a quiet room	15
	(d) Cannot hear well enough to understand someone talking in a normal voice in a quiet room	10
	(e) Cannot hear well enough to understand someone talking in a normal voice on a busy street	8
	(f) No problem with hearing	0

Activity	Descriptor	Points
12. Vision in normal daylight or bright electric light with glasses or other aid to vision if such aid is normally worn	(a) Cannot tell light from dark	15
	(b) Cannot see the shape of furniture in the room	15
	(c) Cannot see well enough to read 16 point print at a distance greater than 20 centimetres	15
	(d) Cannot see well enough to recognise a friend across the room at a distance of at least 5 metres	12
	(e) Cannot see well enough to recognise a friend across the road at a distance of at least 15 metres	8
	(f) No problems with vision	0
13. Continence (other than enuresis)	(a) No voluntary control over bowels	15
	(b) No voluntary control over bladder	15
	(c) Loses control of bowels at least once a week	15
	(d) Loses control of bowels at least once a month	15
	(e) Loses control of bowels occasionally	9
	(f) Loses control of bladder at least once a month	3
	(g) Loses control of bladder occasionally	0
	(h) No problem with continence	0
14. Remaining conscious without having epileptic or similar seizures during waking moments	(a) Has an involuntary episode of lost or altered consciousness at least once a day	15
	(b) Has an involuntary episode of lost or altered consciousness at least once a week	15
	(c) Has an involuntary episode of lost or altered consciousness at least once a month	15
	(d) Has had an involuntary episode of lost or altered consciousness at least twice in the 6 months before the day in respect to which it falls to be determined incapable of work for the purposes of entitlement to any benefit, allowance or advantage	12

Activity	Descriptor	Points
14. (continued)	(e) Has had an involuntary episode of lost or altered consciousness once in the 6 months before the day in respect to which it falls to be determined incapable of work for the purposes of entitlement to any benefit, allowance or advantage	8
	(f) Has had an involuntary episode of lost or altered consciousness once in the 3 years before the day in respect to which it falls to be determined incapable of work for the purposes of entitlement to any benefit, allowance or advantage	0
	(g) Has no problems with consciousness	0

Mental illness and learning disabilities

Activity	Descriptor	Points
15. Completion of tasks	(a) Cannot answer the telephone and reliably take a message	2
	(b) Often sits for hours doing nothing	2
	(c) Cannot concentrate to read a magazine article or follow a radio or television programme	1
	(d) Cannot use a telephone book or other directory to find a number	1
	(e) Mental condition prevents undertaking leisure activities previously enjoyed	1
	(f) Overlooks or forgets the risk posed by domestic appliances or other common hazards due to poor concentration	1
	(g) Agitation, confusion or forgetfulness has resulted in potentially dangerous accidents in the 3 months before the day in respect to which it falls to be determined incapable of work for the purposes of entitlement to any benefit, allowance or advantage.	1
	(h) Concentration can only be sustained by prompting	1
16. Daily living	(a) Needs encouragement to get up and dress	2
	(b) Needs alcohol before midday	2
	(c) Is frequently distressed at some time of the day due to fluctuation of mood	1
	(d) Does not care about his appearance and living conditions	1
	(e) Sleep problems interfere with his daytime activities	1
17. Coping with pressure	(a) Mental stress was a factor in having to stop work	2

Activity	Descriptor	Points
17. (continued)	(b) Frequently feels scared or panicky for no obvious reason	2
	(c) Avoids carrying out routine activities because convinced they will prove too tiring or stressful	1
	(d) Is unable to cope with changes in daily routine	1
	(e) Frequently finds there are so many things to do so gives up because of fatigue, apathy or disinterest	1
	(f) Is scared or anxious that work would bring back or worsen illness	1
18. Interaction with other people	(a) Cannot look after self without help from others	2
	(b) Gets upset by ordinary events resulting in disruptive behavioural problems	2
	(c) Mental problems impair ability to communicate with other people	2
	(d) Gets irritated by things that would not have been a problem before illness	1
	(e) Prefers to be left alone for 6 hours or more each day	1
	(f) Is too frightened to go out alone	1

Weekly benefit rates: 2004 / 2005

Means tested benefits

Income Support & Income-Based Jobseeker's Allowance

Single person, under 18	lower rate	33.50
	higher rate	44.05
Single person, aged 18 – 24		44.05
Single person, aged 25 +		55.65
Lone parent, under 18	lower rate	33.50
	higher rate	44.05
Lone parent, aged 18 +		55.65
Couple, both under 18		33.50 / 44.05 / 66.50
Couple, one under 18		44.05 / 55.65 / 87.30
Couple,		87.30
Dependant children*		42.27

Premiums

Bereavement	23.95
Carer	25.55
Disability, single	23.70
Disability, couple	33.85
Disabled Child*	42.49
Enhanced Disability, single person / lone parent	11.60
Enhanced Disability, couple	16.75
Family *	15.95
Family, lone parent**	15.90
Pensioner, single (JSA only)	49.80
Pensioner, couple	73.65
Severe Disability, per qualifying person	44.15

Housing Benefit & Council Tax Benefit

As for Income Support / Income-Based JSA or Pension Credit, except for:

Personal Allowances	
Single person, under 18 (n/a for Council Tax Benefit)	44.05
Single person, aged 60 – 64	105.45
Single person, aged 65 +	121.00
Lone parent, under 18 (n/a for CTB)	44.05
Couple, both under 18 (n/a for CTB)	66.50
Couple, one or both aged 65 +	181.20
Couple, one or both aged 60-64	160.95

Premiums

Family, old lone parent rate	22.20
Family,	15.95
Family, baby rate	10.50

Working Tax Credit (annual rates)

Basic element	1570
Couple / lone parent	1545
30 hours element	640
Disability element	2100
Severe disability element	890
50 + return to work, 16-29 hours	1075
50 + return to work, 30 + hours	1610
Childcare costs, one child (up to 70% of)	135(pw)
Childcare costs, two children (up to 70% of)	200 (pw)

Child Tax Credit

Family element	545
Baby addition	545
Child element	1625
Disabled child	2215
Severely disabled child	890

Non means tested benefit

Attendance Allowance	lower rate	39.35
	higher rate	58.80

Bereavement Benefits[c]

Bereavement Allowance	79.60
Widowed Parent's Allowance	79.60
Widowed Parent's Allowance, child dependant	11.35[d]
Bereavement Payment (lump sum)	2000

Carer's Allowance

Carers Allowance	44.35
Carers Allowance, adult dependant	26.50
Carers Allowance, child dependant	11.35[d]

Child Benefit

Only / eldest child	16.50
Old lone parent rate**	17.55
Other children	11.05

Disability Living Allowance

Care Component	lower rate	15.55
	middle rate	39.35
	higher rate	58.80
Mobility Component	lower rate	15.55
	higher rate	41.05

Incapacity Benefit

Short term (under pension age)	lower rate	55.90
	higher rate	66.15
Child dependant (paid with higher rate)		11.35[d]
Short term (under pension age) adult dependant		34.60
Long term		74.15
Long term, age addition	lower rate (under 35)	7.80
	higher rate (35 – 44)	15.55
Long term, adult dependant		44.35
Long term, child dependant		11.35[d]
Long term inv. allowance		
	lower rate	5.00
	middle rate	10.00
	higher rate	15.55

Industrial Injuries Disablement Benefit

(Variable depending on % disablement)

Under 18	14.71 – 73.55
Under 18 with dependants	24.02 – 120.10
Aged 18 +	24.02 – 120.10

Jobseeker's Allowance

Under 18	33.50
Aged 18 – 24	44.05
Aged 25 +	55.65

Maternity Allowance

Standard rate	102.80
Adult Dependant	34.60

Severe Disablement Allowance

Severe Disablement Allowance		44.80
Age addition	lower rate (aged 50 –59)	4.85
	middle rate (aged 40-49)	10.00
	higher rate (aged under 40)	15.55
Adult dependant		26.65
Child dependant		11.35[d]

Statutory Maternity, Paternity & Adoption Pay	102.80
Statutory Sick Pay	66.15

National Minimum Wage

(per hour)

	Oct '03	Oct '04
Aged 22+	£4.50	£4.85
Aged 18 – 21 or in approved training	£3.80	£4.10
Aged 16 –18	-	£3.00

c Widow's Pension & Widowed mother's Allowance paid at same rates

d Reduced where CB is payable. Replaced b Child Tax Credit for new claimants

* For existing claims at 12th April 2004

** For those receiving from 5th July 1998

Useful Contacts

Care

Carers Online

Carers Online is a partnership website. It provides carers, those supporting them and others with national and local information. National information on the site is provided by Carers UK.

www.carersonline.org.uk

Elders

Age Concern

Age Concern supports all people over 50 in the UK, ensuring that they get the most from life. They provide essential services such as day care and information. They also campaign on issues like age discrimination and pensions, and work to influence public opinion and government policy about older people.

If you are unable to find the required information on the website, www.ageconcern.org.uk, wherever you are based in the UK you can call:

Age Concern Information Line: 0800 00 99 66

It can help with a wealth of information on Community Care, Health, Income & Benefits, Housing, and Consumer Issues affecting older people. Telephone lines are open from 7 am to 7 pm, 365 days a year.

Those who are hard of hearing can contact the Info Line via Typetalk.

They operate nationally from four offices based in England, Wales, Scotland and Northern Ireland.

Age Concern England

Astral House
1268 London Road
London SW16 4ER
For general enquiries you can call 020 8765 7200

Age Concern Cymru

1 Cathedral Road
Cardiff
CF11 9SD
Tel: (029) 2037 1566
Fax: (029) 2039 9562
Email: enquiries@accymru.org.uk
www.accymru.org.uk

Age Concern Scotland

Leonard Small House
113 Rose Street
Edinburgh
EH2 3DT
Telephone: 0131 220 3345
Fax: 0131 220 2779
Freephone: 0800 00 99 66 (7am - 7pm, 7 days a week)
Email: enquiries@acscot.org.uk
www.ageconcernscotland.org.uk

Age Concern Northern Ireland

3 Lower Crescent Belfast BT7 1NR
Tel: +44(0)28 9024 5729
Fax: +44(0)28 9023 5479
Email: info@ageconcernni.org

Help the Aged

Help the Aged funds and offers a range of services to older people, ensuring greater independence and peace of mind, both inside and outside the home.

They offer SeniorLine, which is a free telephone advice service, that aims to promote independence by offering advice or information on a wide range of welfare rights issues, including claiming benefits or entitlements, housing advice, getting help at home, and entitlement to a bus pass.

Telephone SeniorLine: 0808 800 6565
Lines are open Monday to Friday 9am-4pm
www.helptheaged.org.uk

Equality

Disability Rights Commission

The DRC is an independent body set up by the Government to help secure civil rights for disabled people. They have produced some free guidance booklets that outline responsibilities in brief and guidelines for people with disabilities to follow if they believe they have been discriminated against. The DRC has also published codes of practice, regulations, and guidance to assist both people with disabilities and employers / service providers. These are all available from the DRC website or through the Helpline.

If these are followed they may aid employers and service providers in meeting their responsibilities under the Act or at least demonstrate that they are thinking positively about eliminating barriers for people with disabilities.

The DRC helpline provides information and advice about all aspects of the Disability Discrimination Act, as well it can offer good practice advice on the employment of disabled people. It is open from 8am to 8pm Monday to Friday.

Tel: 08457 622 633
Fax: 08457 778 878
Textpost: 08457 622 644
Freepost MID: 02164
Straford-upon-Avon CV37 9HY
Email: enquiry@drc-gb.org
Website: www.drc-gb.org

Equal Opportunities Commission

The EOC was set up as an independent statutory body with the following powers:

- to work towards the elimination of discrimination on the grounds of sex or marriage
- to promote equality of opportunity for women and men
- to keep under review the Sex Discrimination Act and the Equal Pay Act.

It provides up-to-date advice on rights and produces straightforward information to help individuals and employers. It offers a helpline to the public. Call 08456 015 901. Visit the website at www.eoc.org.uk.

Jobs

Jobseeker Direct telephone helpline

This helpline is available to anyone who is looking for work and will help you to find part-time or full-time work. Your call is charged at local rate no matter where in the country you phone from. It is open from 9.00am until 6.00pm on weekdays and from 9.00am until 1.00pm on Saturdays. The telephone number is 0845 6060 234 and the textphone is 0845 6055 255.

Department for Work and Pensions

The Department for Work and Pensions can be contacted at www.dwp.gov.uk or from 9.00am to 5.00pm Monday to Friday on 020 7712 2171.

Jobcentre Plus

The Jobcentre Plus website is www.jobcentreplus.gov.uk. Details of all local Jobcentre Plus offices can be found there.

Jobability.com

Jobability.com is a job website for disabled people. It has been set up in direct response to the Disability Rights Commission's (DRC) Actions Speak Louder Than Words initiative.

The project is run as a three-way partnership between Microsoft, Leonard Cheshire and totaljobs.com.

The website is www.jobability.com

Employers' Forum on Disability

The Forum is recognised as an authoritative voice on disability as it affects employers and service providers.

The Forum works closely with government and other stakeholders, sharing best practice to make it easier to employ disabled people and serve disabled customers.

The website wwww.employers-forum.co.uk also provides statistical information and research findings about disabled people, and links into other recommended sites for proactive job searches.

Other

Action for Blind People

Action for Blind People's Welfare Rights Service aims to guide visually impaired people and their advisers through the benefits maze. Factsheets, benefit briefings, checklists, frequently asked questions, and news articles can be opened or downloaded from their website, www.afbp.org.

Action for Blind People
14-16 Verney Road
London
SE16 3DZ
Telephone: 020 7635 4800
Fax: 020 7635 4900
Email: info@afbp.org
Information & Advice Service National Helpline 0800 915 4666

Neath Mind's Benefits and Mental Health Website

The website identifies benefits that you might be entitled to, how to claim them and how to support others with benefit claims.

www.benefitsinmind.org.uk

The National Debtline

The National Debtline is a national telephone helpline for people with debt problems in England, Wales and Scotland. The service is free, confidential and independent.

The specialist advice given over the telephone is backed up with written self-help materials, which are free. If your circumstances meet certain criteria they can, if you are interested, assist in setting up a Debt Management Plan for you, also for free.

Opening times are: Monday - Friday 9am-9pm and Saturday 9.30am - 1pm

Telephone: 0808 808 4000
www.nationaldebtline.co.uk

Free Booklets

DLE7 Employing Disabled People – A Good Practice Guide for Managers and Employers

DL170 What Employers Need to Know

DX25 Good Practice Training Directory

FOCUS6 Good Signs for Service Providers – Improving Signs for People with a Learning Disability

FOCUS Guidance on providing BSL and English Interpreter under the DDA

EMPS How do I make a claim? A guide to taking a DDA Case to an Employment Tribunal

EQU1 Quality and Disability – Equality in the Best Value Regime

DL200 Some Useful Suggestions

DLE3 What Employees and Job Applicants Need to Know

COPSCH Code of Practice for Schools - (Part 1)

COPSCH Code of Practice for Schools – (Part 2)

COPP16 Code of Practice: Post 16 Education and Related Services (Part 1)

EDU A Guide for Disabled Students and Learners

Guidance on Matters to be taken into Account in Determining Questions Relating to the Definition of Disability

Code of Practice for the Elimination of Discrimination in the Field of Employment against Disabled Persons or Persons who have had a Disability

Codes of Practice on Employment and Occupation – to be published prior to 1 October 2004 and replace the above code.

More guidance for Employers regarding Part 2 of the DDA 1995 can be found at www.drc-gb.org under the Employers and Service, Employment Section.

Code of Practice – Duties of Trade Organisations to their Disabled Members and Applicants.

Code of Practice For Trade Organisations and Qualifications Bodies – to be published prior to 1 October 2004 and replace the above code.

Code of Practice (revised) – Rights of Access Goods Facilities Services and Premises.

More guidance can be found for Service providers, for Part 3 of the DDA, at www.drc-gb.org, under the Employers and Service, Access to Service section.

Code of Practice for Schools – DDA 1995 Part 4

Code of Practice for Providers of Post 16 Education and Related Services – DDA 1995 Part 4

Everything you need to know about education and how education bodies can meet their requirements under Part 4 of the DDA 1995, can be found at www.drc-gb.org, under the Employers and Service, Education Section.

Benefits Law, Regulations and Other Sources

There are several Acts of Parliament governing Social Security and a large number of regulations that also have the force of law. The legislation has been greatly amended and you can find it on the DWP website at www.dwp.gov.uk/advisers/docs/-lawvols/bluevol/ index.asp. They may also be available in a good public library or you can ask to see them at a DWP office (that may know them as the Blue Volumes).

The Decision Maker's Guide is the DWP's internal guidance for staff on how to deal with benefit claims. It is available at DWP offices and on their website at www.dwp.gov.uk/publications/dwp/dmg/.

There are a number of other internal DWP guidance manuals including guidance on disability, guidance to doctors about incapacity for work, and the Social Fund. These are also available on the DWP's website.

If you do not have access to the Internet or prefer not to use it then you can make an appointment with your local Jobcentre Plus office and they will let you read them. If you have any problems you should ask to speak to the manager or customer services and if they are not helpful you can contact your MP who could negotiate on your behalf.

The Housing Benefit Guidance Manual is held by local authorities and you can ask to use a copy at your local council. It is also available on-line at www.dwp.gov.uk/housingbenefit/manuals/index.asp.

Code of Practice for the Elimination of Discrimination in the Field of Employment against Disabled Persons or Persons who have had a Disability and, from October 1 2004 its replacement, the Code of Practice on Employment and Occupation

Guidance for Employers regarding Part 2 of the DDA 1995 can be found at www.drc-gb.org, under the Employers and Service, Employment Section. More guidance can be found for Service Providers for Part 3 of the DDA, under the Employers and Service, Access to Service section, and for Part 4 (about education and how education bodies can meet their requirements) under the Employers and Service, Education Section.

Code of Practice – Duties of Trade Organisations to their Disabled Members and Applicants and the Code of Practice for Trade Organisations and Qualifications Bodies – to be published prior to 1 October 2004 and replace the above code.

Code of Practice (revised) – Rights of Access; Goods, Facilities, Services and Premises

Code of Practice for Schools – DDA 1995 Part 4

Code of Practice for Providers of Post 16 Education and Related Services – DDA 1995 Part 4

The key regulations include:

The Disability Discrimination (Meaning of Disability) Regulations 1996

The Disability Discrimination (Employment) Regulations 1996

The Disability Discrimination (Service and Premises) 1996

The Disability Discrimination (Service and Premises) Regulations 1999

The Disability Discrimination (Providers of Services) (Adjustments of Premises) Regulations 2001

The Disability Discrimination Act 1995 (Taxis) (Carrying of Guide Dogs etc.) (England and Wales) Regulations 2000

The Disability Discrimination (Sub-leases and Sub-tenancies) Regulations 1996

The Disability Discrimination (Questions and Replies) Order 1996

Useful books about benefit rights

The Young Person's Handbook Second Edition, Liz Britton (ed), Centre for Economic & Social Inclusion

Welfare to Work Handbook 2003, Will Somerville (ed), Centre for Economic & Social Inclusion

Welfare to Work Handbook Second Edition, Will Somerville and Chris Brace (ed), Centre for Economic & Social Inclusion

Disability Rights Handbook 2004-05, Disability Alliance

The Welfare Benefits and Tax Credits Handbook 2004 –05, Child Poverty Action Group

Guide to Housing Benefit and Council Tax Benefit 2004–05, Shelter and the Chartered Institute of Housing

Paying for Care Handbook, Child Poverty Action Group

Migration and Social Security Handbook, Child Poverty Action Group

Debt Advice Handbook, Child Poverty Action Group

Useful Websites (see free CD Rom)

Child Poverty Action Group www.cpag.org.uk

Citizens Advice Adviceguide www.adviceguide.org.uk

Community Legal Service leaflets www.clsdirect.org.uk

Coventry Law Centre – leaflets about discrimination and employment www.covlaw.org.uk/employment/leaflets

DIAL UK www.dial.org.uk

Shelternet www.shelternet.org.uk

Mencap www.askmencap.info

After 16 www.after16.org.uk

Barton Hill Advice Centre – guides to claiming benefits www.bhas.org.uk

Disability Rights Commission www.drc-gb.org

Disability Alliance www.disabilityalliance.org (large number of links to useful websites on a wide range of disability related topics)

UK Ability www.ukability.co.uk

Scope www.scope.org.uk

Department for Work and Pensions, Disability Unit www.disability.gov.uk

Department for Work and Pensions www.dwp.gov.uk

Department for Education and Skills www.dfes.gov.uk

Inland Revenue www.inlandrevenue.gov.uk

Jobcentre Plus www.jobcentreplus.gov.uk

Rightsnet www.rightsnet.org.uk

Other sources

Budget Report 2004

Budget Statement, Chapter 4 – 'Increasing Employment Opportunity For All', April 2003

Budget Statement, Chapter 4 - 'Increasing Employment Opportunity For All', April 2004

Business on Board, New Deal Task Force, July 2001

Carers (ISBN 011 621 555), Office for National Statistics, February 2000

DWP In-house report 128: A review of disability estimates and definitions, March 2004

DWP leaflets. There are large number of leaflets published by the DWP and the Inland Revenue. These are available on their websites from DWP and Inland Revenue offices or by phoning 0845 602 4444 (DWP).

Improving the Life Chances of Disabled People: Interim Analytical Report, Prime Minister's Strategy Unit

Jobcentre Plus Programmes Guide, Jobcentre Plus, 2002

Jobcentre Plus Programmes Guide, Jobcentre Plus, 2003

Office for National Statistics - CARERS 2000 (ISBN 011 621 555)

Pathways to Work: Helping People Into Employment, Green Paper, November 2002

Prime Minister's Strategy Unit - Improving the Life Chances of Disabled People: Interim Analytical Report

Procedural guidance for all the employment programmes, Jobcentre Plus and DWP, 2003

Spending Review 2002

Work Focused Interview Procedural Guidance, Department for Work & Pensions, Version 5, April 2003

Author Biographies

Neil Bateman (Editor)

Neil Bateman is a writer, trainer and consultant who specialises in welfare rights and social policy issues. He has established and managed a local authority welfare rights service, been an established policy adviser to the Local Government Association and his written work has been extensively published. He is also a contributor to other *Inclusion* handbooks. More information is available at www.neilbateman.co.uk

Will Somerville (Editor)

Will has worked on various projects in the fields of migration, equality, social enterprise and welfare to work. He has edited two editions the Welfare to Work Handbook as well as the Newcomers Handbook. Previous employment includes the Prime Minister's Strategy Unit and the think tank the Institute of Public Policy Research (ippr).

Chris Brace

Chris is *Inclusion*'s Information and Communications Manager. He joined *Inclusion* in January 2003, having previously worked at the Learning and Skills Development Agency and London Guildhall University. He has a Masters Degree in Contemporary British Politics from Goldsmiths University.

Chris has designed the Welfare to Work website (www.w2w.org.uk), and co-ordinates the programme for the Welfare to Work Convention. He has written 'How to employ local people' for Lambeth Council, which outlines into work programmes available to employers in that area. He edits Working Brief, *Inclusion*'s monthly journal.

Abena Dadze-Arthur

Abena Dadze-Arthur is a Policy and Research Officer as well as the Equality and Diversity Officer at *Inclusion*. She has experience of designing and carrying out primary research projects and is trained in the analysis and presentation of both quantitative and qualitative data. Former employment includes being an international Market Researcher.

Kath Hoskisson

Kath has worked in the field of disabilities for the last 11 years after leaving the NHS where she was a Registered General Nurse. She originally set up the 'Sandwell Disability Charter' for Employers and Service Providers in 1998, and as a result achieved the runners up MJ/ADLO Award for Best Community Initiative in 1999 (National Award). Kath also set up and chaired the Sandwell Disability Partnership in 1997 for 6 years, before going on to manage the Disability Employment Resource Centre for Sandwell.

She has written the W2WJIP Vision and Action Plan for Sandwell and has worked as a Part Time Disability Consultant with the public in West Bromwich. She has also lectured part time at Guildford University on the Disability Discrimination Act for Post graduate students.

Mark Morrin

Mark Morrin is experienced within the field of economic development and regeneration, managing a wide range of projects, from strategy to implementation, including specialist areas of European funding programmes, community based economic development, social enterprise, and training and employment programmes.

Donnia Reafat

Donnia Reafat has recently joined *Inclusion* as a Research Assistant. Prior to *Inclusion*, Donnia worked for Oxfam GB in the Humanitarian department, contributing to programming activities and evaluations for the Asia and Africa desks. She has also worked as an assistant to the Chief Executive of the disability charity Scope and in the area of policy and grant making at the Association of London Government and The Health Foundation.

Abbreviations

AT	Action Team
AA	Attendance Allowance
BET	Basic Employability Training
CA	Carer's Allowance
CV	Curriculum Vitae
CTB	Council Tax Benefit
CTBRO	Council Tax Benefit Run On
CTC	Child Tax Credit
DEA	Disability Employment Adviser
DDA	Disability Discrimination Act
DfES	Department for Education and Skills
DLA	Disability Living Allowance
DM	Decision Maker
DMG	Decision Maker's Guide
DMA	Decision Making and Appeals
DRC	Disability Rights Commission
DWP	Department for Work and Pensions
EEA	European Economic Area
EEC	European Economic Community
ESF	European Social Fund
ETF	Environment Task Force
ETO	Education and Training Opportunities
EU	European Union
EZ	Employment Zone
FE	Further Education
FTET	Full-time Education and Training
GtW	Gateway to Work
HB	Housing Benefit
HBRO	Housing Benefit Run On
IAP	Individual Action Plan
IB	Incapacity Benefit
IBJSA	Income-Based Jobseeker's Allowance
IS	Income Support

ITP	Individual Training Plan
IWBC	In-work Better Off Calculation
JIS	Job Introduction Scheme
JSA	Jobseeker's Allowance
JSAg	Jobseeker's Agreement
JRRP	Joint Rehabilitation and Retention Pilot
LA	Local Authority
LEA	Local Education Authority
LSC	Learning and Skills Council
LOT	Longer Occupational Training
LPRO	Lone Parent Run On
MA	Modern Apprenticeship
MIC	Music Industry Consultant
MIG	Minimum Income Guarantee
MIRO	Mortgage Interest Run On
MOLP	Musician's Open Learning Pack
ND25+	New Deal 25 Plus
ND50+	New Deal 50 Plus
NDDP	New Deal for Disabled Partner
NDLP	New Deal for Lone Parents
NDP	New Deal Partners
NDPA	New Deal personal adviser
NDYP	New Deal for Young People
NI	National Insurance
NVQ	National Vocational Qualification
Ofsted	Office for Standards in Education
PC	Pension Credit
PCA	Personal Capability Assessment
PIW	Period of Interruption of Work
PSA	Public Service Agreement
REA	Reduced Earnings Allowance
RTWC	Return to Work Credit
RDA	Regional Development Agency
SDA	Severe Disability Allowance

SENDA	Special Educational Needs and Disability Act 2001
SEP	Self-Employed Provision
SJFT	Short Job Focused Training
SoS	Secretary of State
SRB	Single Regeneration Budget
SSC	Sector Skills Council
SVQ	Scottish Vocational Qualification
TfW	Training for Work
WBL	Work Based Learning
WBLA	Work Based Learning for Adults
WFI	Work-Focused Interview
WTC	Working Tax Credit

CD-ROM Software Requirements:

The progam on the attached CD-ROM requires web browser software, such as Internet Explorer or Netscape Navigator, to be installed on your computer. You will also need Acrobat Reader to view the electronic version of the handbook and we have included a link within the CD for you to download this free software from their website at *www.adobe.co.uk* if it is not currently installed on your computer.

CD-ROM Installation Instructions:

For Windows 95/98/NT4/ME/2000/XP:

Insert the CD into the CD-ROM drive. The program should start automatically.

Manual installation:

If the CD does not start automatically you can start it manually by doing one of the following:

Click on My Computer, double click on the CD-ROM Drive and double click on the file called 'index.htm' contained on the CD.

Alternatively you can browse for the CD-ROM drive using Windows Explorer and double-click on the file 'index.htm'.

For Apple Mac Computers:

Insert the CD into the CD-ROM drive and Double-click on the CD-ROM icon when it appears on the desktop. Double-click on the file 'index.htm'.

Please note the Centre for Economic and Social Inclusion cannot provide technical support for this CD-ROM.